PROTEST
NATION

ALSO EDITED BY TIMOTHY PATRICK McCARTHY
AND JOHN McMILLIAN

The Radical Reader: A Documentary History of the American Radical Tradition

PROTEST

Words That Inspired a Century

NATION

of American Radicalism

Edited by Timothy Patrick McCarthy

and John McMillian

THE NEW PRESS

NEW YORK
LONDON

Requests for permission to reproduce selections from this book should
be mailed to: Permissions Department, The New Press, 38 Greene Street,
New York, NY 10013.

Published in the United States by The New Press, New York, 2010
Distributed by Perseus Distribution

LIBRARY OF CONGRESS CATALOGING-IN-PUBLICATION DATA

Protest nation : words that inspired a century of American radicalism /
edited by Timothy Patrick McCarthy and John McMillian.
p.   cm.
Includes bibliographical references.
ISBN 978-1-59558-504-2 (pb)
1. Radicalism—United States—History—20th century—
Sources. 2. Protest movements—United States—History—20th
century—Sources. I. McCarthy, Timothy Patrick.
II. McMillian, John Campbell.
HN90.R3P74 2010
303.48'4—dc22
2010003507

The New Press was established in 1990 as a not-for-profit alternative to
the large, commercial publishing houses currently dominating the book
publishing industry. The New Press operates in the public interest rather
than for private gain, and is committed to publishing, in innovative ways,
works of educational, cultural, and community value that are often
deemed insufficiently profitable.

www.thenewpress.com

Composition by Westchester Book Composition

Printed in the United States of America

2   4   6   8   10   9   7   5   3   1

For Howard Zinn (1922–2010):
beloved historian, radical patriot, cherished mentor,
and dear friend

May you finally know peace

Contents

Acknowledgments

Once again, we start by thanking each other—for a rare friendship that's now well into its second decade. What a ride! We would also like to thank our good friends at The New Press, especially our editor Marc Favreau, whose support is outdone only by his patience, which rivals that of Job. Thanks, too, to Maury Botton and Shannon Waite for their hard work in getting this book to press. Special thanks to Eric Foner, for putting us in touch with The New Press a decade ago, and for generally having our back ever since. We also appreciate the ongoing support we get from our other mentors—Harry Reid, Manning Marable, Alan Brinkley, Bob Hanning, and Martin Duberman—and from our colleagues and students at Harvard, especially in History and Literature, Quincy House, and the Carr Center for Human Rights Policy. We continue to be very grateful for the longstanding friendships we share with Jeremy Varon, Mike Foley, Steve Biel, Zoe Trodd, Lizzie and Toby Simon, Renee Richardson Gosline, Richard Parker, and Jeanne Follansbee Quinn. And finally, we want to thank our families and loved ones—Judy and Harlon McMillian, Tom and Michelle McCarthy, Malcolm and Malia Green, and C.J. Crowder—for pushing us and loving us, even when we test the limits. We love you right back.

As this book was going to press, we received the sad news that our friend and mentor Howard Zinn had passed away. We dedicate this book to him, even as we re-dedicate ourselves to the work he inspired so many of us to do.

INTRODUCTION

Timothy Patrick McCarthy
and John McMillian

America is a protest nation. From the Declaration of Independence to the historic election of President Barack Hussein Obama, the politics and culture of the United States have been profoundly shaped by small acts of protest and mass mobilizations for social change. Such dissent has come in a wide variety of forms—it can be conservative or progressive, sweeping or incremental, violent or peaceful, individual or collective. More often than not, American radicalism has drawn its inspiration from the nation's revolutionary founding claims of liberty, equality, and the rights of citizenship. Though these ideals mean different things to different people, they have always helped to animate American political debates and social conflicts. And each generation has made its own contribution to the American radical tradition.

Still, to refer to someone or something as "radical" is to risk offense. To self-identify as such is almost certainly to ensure one's marginalization, to court caricature. Despite the fact that "radical" can reasonably be defined as "going to the root of things," it is more commonly interpreted as "drastic" or "extreme." Radicals are those who decry the status quo, who demand fundamental change, who seek transformation. These kinds of people almost always make others nervous, especially those in power. Without them, however, real social change is much harder to achieve.

The last generation or so has been a fascinating period for historians of American radicalism. Reckless Reaganomics paved the way for a disappointing decade of Clintonian compromise, flanked as it was by two Bush presidencies, the second much more awful than the first. When we were preparing our first book—*The Radical Reader*—back in 2003, the United States had recently invaded Iraq, and George W. Bush had just addressed the nation from a perch on the *USS Abraham Lincoln*, beneath a banner that read "Mission Accomplished." Back then, it wasn't hard to be pessimistic about the direction in which the country was heading. As we took to the streets to protest the war, we had a foreboding sense of doom. But even in our most cynical imaginations, we could not have envisioned the degree to which Bush Administration policies would prove disastrous to so many people across the globe. Our frustration was compounded when the tragedies of the Bush era failed to produce a countervailing social movement of the type that roiled America in the 1960s. Though we were too young to have lived through "the Sixties," we still held out hope that our generation would muster the same bold, sustained spirit of rebellion that characterized that age. The Obama campaign offered a glimmer of hope to a country that had lost its way. Young people, especially, began to believe in something again. But the jury is still out on whether America's first black president will help to bring about the far-reaching change so many of us still believe in.

Protest Nation helps us to understand the important role that radicalism has played in modern American history. This rich collection of sources from the twentieth century both documents and illuminates the radical roots of contemporary America's most progressive thinking. Here you will find inspiring speeches by Eugene Debs, Huey Long, Malcolm X, and Harvey Milk; protest literature written by Upton Sinclair, Charlotte Perkins Gilman, Allen Ginsberg, and Rachel Carson; intellectual masterpieces by Herbert Marcuse, Martin Luther King, Jr., Noam Chomsky, and Audre Lorde; and bold manifestos that helped to launch the New Left, modern feminism, the Black Panther Party, gay liberation, and the American Indian Movement, among others. We begin this book with an excerpt from *The Jungle*

(1905) to emphasize that socialism has a longer history in the United States than many Americans would perhaps like to admit.

The history documented in this book constitutes a field manual of sorts for the contemporary culture wars. Nowadays, we *are* living amidst an insurgent radical movement, only this time it largely derives from the right. Inspired by the noisy rhetoric of media elites such as Rush Limbaugh, Sean Hannity, Ann Coulter, Michelle Malkin, and the truly terrifying Glenn Beck, its rank-and-file embodies a peculiar blend of nationalism and anti-government conspiracy theories, evangelical fervor, and xenophobic bigotry. They invoke God and carry guns. They see an America that is changing rapidly—one where white men must learn to share power and social status with women and minorities; where demands for gay and lesbian equality are gaining visibility and support, especially from the younger generations; and where the Oval Office is occupied by a man who is not only African American, but also cosmopolitan, intellectual, stylish, and sophisticated. Frightened by these new realities—which progressive social movements have helped to bring about—they carry signs that say: "We Want Our Country Back."

But the rest of us deserve to have our history back. Curiously, some of these right-wing populists claim to be working in the tradition of Thomas Paine, though they would be hard pressed to identify any specific commonalities of outlook and purpose between themselves and the eighteenth-century deist (who, of course, is far more accurately embraced as an ancestor to left-wing radicals). Others have sought to link President Obama to Socialism, Communism, Nazism, Fascism, and the Vietnam-era antiwar movement (in which case he's portrayed as either a wimpy peacenik or a bomb-chucking revolutionary). Even the most general student of history should be able to recognize how muddleheaded these designations are, especially when directed simultaneously at a single individual. They succeed, however, in illustrating the need for an enhanced understanding of the radical roots of modern America.

Though we still look forward to the day when progressive forms of radicalism will gather enough strength and cohesion to challenge the power of the radical right, we are nonetheless buoyed by what seems to be a wider cultural recognition and acceptance of the place of radicalism in American politics and society. In this respect, the 2008 election—so full of historic firsts—may well have been a turning point, a profound cultural shift as well as a generational passing of the torch. Throughout the election, President Obama's opponents—both in his own party and way outside of it—tried to portray him as different or foreign, unacceptable in a host of ways. And while this "othering" often took on a predictable racial gloss, it was also an attempt to make him appear too radical by calling attention to his associations with an *angry* black minister, an *anti-American* education professor, *foreign-born* Muslims, and even his supposedly *unpatriotic* wife. That these attempts to "radicalize" Obama failed to sink his candidacy says at least as much about the shifting perception of radicalism in our culture—our evolving ability to discern real threats from imagined ones—as it does about Obama's political skill. Or so we hope.

Several years ago, in an attempt to trace the influence of radicalism in American society, we began making a list of things that radicals have achieved over time. They include: the American Revolution, the abolition of slavery, public education, universal suffrage, public parks, integration, co-education, freedom of speech and assembly, the eight-hour workday, food and drug regulations, the minimum wage, child and prison labor laws, health and safety standards, reproductive choice, same-sex partner benefits, marriage equality, blues, jazz, rock and roll, hip hop, unemployment insurance, HIV/AIDS research, the right to a fair trial, public health clinics, Head Start programs, immigrant rights, collective bargaining, affirmative action, wildlife reserves, clean air and water, African-American studies, and the living wage. It's an impressive, albeit incomplete, list, and it underscores the point that America would be a far less decent and less democratic place were it not for the work of activists who have struggled to make real America's founding promises of freedom and equality.

As we begin the next American century—one with unmistakably global implications—it is worth remembering that many of the things we now take for granted have radical roots. It is also worth noting that radical thinking and action can be valuable regardless of their degree of influence. In times of great crisis and repression—the likes of which we have experienced recently—citizens may find it worthwhile to simply speak their minds, demand their rights, dream of a different world, and work to bring it about. As Margaret Mead exhorted us: "Never doubt that a small group of thoughtful, committed citizens can change the world. Indeed, it is the only thing that ever has." Democracy is not inevitable. As we have seen again in recent years, it cannot be imposed from on high; it must be generated from below. In these precarious times, we need to remember that freedom and equality have never been given freely or distributed equally—in America or anywhere else.

1. UPTON SINCLAIR

The Jungle
(1905)

Among the most celebrated accomplishment of muckraking journalism in the early twentieth century was **UPTON SINCLAIR**'s *The Jungle*, which began appearing serially in the socialist weekly *Appeal to Reason* in early 1905. Sinclair (1878–1968) attended the College of the City of New York and Columbia University, and spent much of his life gravitating in and out of the American Socialist Party. Over the course of his career, he published more than eighty books, many of which helped to lay the groundwork for social and industrial reforms. Although Sinclair won the 1943 Pulitzer Prize in fiction for the novel *Dragon's Teeth*, he is best known for *The Jungle*, a sociological "novel" that exposed the grotesque conditions in Chicago stockyards and led to the passage of federal food inspection laws. Sinclair, however, was disappointed with the book's reception. Dedicated "To the Workingmen of America," *The Jungle* was intended to be a critique of the new industrial order, and was only secondarily about the unsanitary conditions in Chicago stockyards. Wrote Sinclair, "I aimed at the public's heart, and by accident I hit it in the stomach."

SOURCE: Upton Sinclair. *The Jungle*. New York: Doubleday, 1906.

SELECTED READINGS: Leon Harris, *Upton Sinclair, American Rebel* (1975). Upton Sinclair, *Autobiography* (1962).

Jurgis heard of these things little by little, in the gossip of those who were obliged to perpetrate them. It seemed as if every time you met a person from a new department, you heard of new swindles and new crimes. There was, for instance, a Lithuanian who was a cattle butcher for the plant where Marija had worked, which killed meat for canning only; and to hear this man describe the animals which came to his place would have been worth while for a Dante or a Zola. It seemed that they must have agencies all over the country, to hunt out old and crippled and diseased cattle to be canned. There were cattle which had been fed on "whisky-malt," the refuse of the breweries, and had become what the men called "steerly"—which means covered with boils. It was a nasty job killing these, for when you plunged your knife into them they would burst and splash foul-smelling stuff into your face; and when a man's sleeves were smeared with blood, and his hands steeped in it, how was he ever to wipe his face, or to clear his eyes so that he could see? It was stuff such as this that made the "embalmed beef" that had killed several times as many United States soldiers as all the bullets of the Spaniards; only the army beef, besides, was not fresh canned; it was old stuff that had been lying for years in the cellars.

Then one Sunday evening, Jurgis sat puffing his pipe by the kitchen stove, and talking with an old fellow whom Jonas had introduced, and who worked in the canning rooms at Durham's; and so Jurgis learned a few things about the great and only Durham canned goods, which had become a national institution. They were regular alchemists at Durham's; they advertised a mushroom-catsup, and the men who made it did not know what a mushroom looked like. They advertised "potted chicken,"—and it was like the boarding-house soup of the comic papers, through which a chicken had walked with rubbers on. Perhaps they had a secret process for making chickens chemically—who knows? said Jurgis' friend; the things that went into the mixture were tripe, and the fat of pork, and beef suet, and hearts of beef, and finally the waste ends of veal, when they had any. They put these up in several grades, and sold them at several prices; but the contents of the cans all came out of the same hopper. And then there was "potted game" and "potted grouse," "potted ham," and "deviled ham"—de-vyled, as the men called it. "De-vyled" ham was made out of the waste ends of smoked beef that were too small to be sliced by the machines; and also tripe, dyed with chemicals so that it would not show white; and trimmings of hams and corned beef; and potatoes, skins and all; and finally the hard cartilaginous gullets of beef, after the tongues had been cut out. All this ingenious mixture was ground up and flavored with spices to make it taste like something. Anybody who could invent a new imitation had been sure of a fortune from old Durham, said Jurgis' informant; but it was hard to think of anything new in a place where so many sharp wits had been at work for so long; where men welcomed tuberculosis in the cattle they were feeding, because it made them fatten more quickly; and where they bought up all the old rancid butter left over in the grocery stores of a continent, and "oxidized" it by a forced-air process, to take away the odor, rechurned it with skim milk, and sold it in bricks in the cities! Up to a year or two ago it had been the custom to kill horses in the yards—ostensibly for fertilizer; but after long agitation the newspapers had been able to make the public realize that the horses were being canned. Now it was against the law to kill horses in Packingtown, and the law was really complied with—for the present, at any rate. Any day, however, one might see sharp-horned and shaggy-haired creatures running with the sheep—and yet what a job you would have to get the public to believe that a good part of what it buys for lamb and mutton is really goat's flesh!

There was another interesting set of statistics that a person might have gathered in Packingtown—those of the various afflictions of the workers. When Jurgis had first inspected the packing plants with Szedvilas, he had marveled while he listened to the tale of all the things that were made out of the carcasses of animals, and of all the lesser industries that were maintained there; now he found that each one of these lesser industries was a separate little inferno, in its way as horrible as the killing beds, the source and fountain of them all. The workers in each of them had their own peculiar diseases. And the wandering visitor might be skeptical about all the swindles, but he could not be skeptical about these, for the worker bore the evidence of them about on his own person—generally he had only to hold out his hand.

There were the men in the pickle rooms, for instance, where old Antanas had gotten his death; scarce a one of these that had not some spot of horror on his person. Let a man so much as scrape his finger pushing a truck in the pickle rooms, and he might have a sore that would put him out of the world; all the joints in his fingers might be eaten by the acid, one by one. Of the butchers and floorsmen, the beef-boners and trimmers, and all those who used knives, you could scarcely find a person who had the use of his thumb; time and time again the base of it had been slashed, till it was a mere lump of flesh against which the man pressed the knife to hold it. The hands of these men would be criss-crossed with cuts, until you could no longer pretend to count them or to trace them. They would have no nails,—they had worn them off pulling hides; their knuckles were swollen so that their fingers spread out like a fan. There were men who worked in the cooking rooms, in the midst of steam and sickening odors, by artificial light; in these rooms the germs of tuberculosis might live for two years, but the supply was renewed every hour. There were the beef-luggers, who carried two-hundred-pound quarters into the refrigerator-cars; a fearful kind of work, that began at four o'clock in the morning, and that wore out the most powerful men in a few years. There were those who worked in the chilling rooms, and whose special disease was rheumatism; the time limit that a man could work in the chilling rooms was said to be five years. There were the wool-pluckers, whose hands went to pieces even sooner than the hands of the pickle men; for the pelts of the sheep had to be painted with acid to loosen the wool, and then the pluckers had to pull out this wool with their bare hands, till the acid had eaten their fingers off. There were those who made the tins for the canned meat; and their hands, too, were a maze of cuts, and each cut represented a chance for blood poisoning. Some worked at the stamping machines, and it was very seldom that one could work long there at the pace that was set, and not give out and forget himself, and have a part of his hand chopped off. There were the "hoisters," as they were called, whose task it was to press the lever which lifted the dead cattle off the floor. They ran along upon a rafter, peering down through the damp and the steam; and as old Durham's architects had not built the killing room for the convenience of the hoisters, at every few feet they would have to stoop under a beam, say four feet above the one they ran on; which got them into the habit of stooping, so that in a few years they would be walking like chimpanzees. Worst of any, however, were the fertilizer men, and those who served in the cooking rooms. These people could not be shown to the visitor,—for the odor of a fertilizer man would scare any ordinary visitor at a hundred yards, and as for the other men, who worked in tank rooms full of steam, and in some of which there were open vats near the level of the floor, their peculiar trouble was that they fell into the vats; and when they were fished out, there was never enough of them left to be worth exhibiting,—sometimes they would be overlooked for days, till all but the bones of them had gone out to the world as Durham's Pure Leaf Lard!

2. EMMA GOLDMAN

Anarchism: What It Really Stands For
(1911)

EMMA GOLDMAN's 1911 essay "Anarchism: What It Really Stands For" aimed to correct popular misapprehensions about anarchism. Goldman (1869–1940) was born in Lithuania and emigrated to Rochester, New York, in 1886. In 1889, she became active in the anarchist movement, and her frequent lectures attracted national attention. In 1906, Goldman and Alexander Berkman began publishing *Mother Earth*, an anarchist magazine of art and social criticism. Goldman was also an early advocate of free speech, birth control, women's independence, and the eight-hour workday. In 1917, she was sentenced to two years in prison for obstructing the draft, and she was deported to Russia immediately after her release in 1919. In this lively essay, Goldman promoted an essentially libertarian philosophy of total individual freedom, arguing that centralized governments crushed individualism and stifled humanity.

SOURCE: Emma Goldman. *Anarchism and Other Essays.* New York: Mother Earth Publishing Association, 1911.

SELECTED READINGS: Peter Glassgold, ed., *Anarchy! An Anthology of Emma Goldman's* Mother Earth (2001). Emma Goldman, *Red Emma Speaks* (1996). Martha Solomon, *Emma Goldman* (1987).

Anarchy

Ever reviled, accursed, ne'er understood,
Thou art the grisly terror of our age.
"Wreck of all order," cry the multitude,
"Art thou, and war and murder's endless rage."
O, let them cry. To them that ne'er have striven
The truth that lies behind a word to find,
To them the word's right meaning was not given.
They shall continue blind among the blind.
But thou, O word, so clear, so strong, so pure,
Thou sayest all which I for goal have taken.
I give thee to the future! Thine secure
When each at least unto himself shall waken.
Comes it in sunshine? In the tempest's thrill?
I cannot tell—but it the earth shall see!
I am an Anarchist! Wherefore I will
Not rule, and also ruled I will not be!

John Henry Mackay

The history of human growth and development is at the same time the history of the terrible struggle of every new idea heralding the approach of a brighter dawn. In its tenacious hold on tradition, the Old has never hesitated to make use of the foulest and cruelest means to stay the advent of the New, in whatever form or period the latter may have asserted itself. Nor need we retrace our steps into the distant past to realize the enormity of opposition, difficulties, and hardships placed in the path of every progressive idea. The rack, the thumbscrew, and the knout are still with us; so are the convict's garb and the social wrath, all conspiring against the spirit that is serenely marching on.

Anarchism could not hope to escape the fate of all other ideas of innovation. Indeed, as the most revolutionary and uncompromising innovator, Anarchism must needs meet with the combined ignorance and venom of the world it aims to reconstruct.

To deal even remotely with all that is being said and done against Anarchism would necessitate the writing of a whole volume. I shall therefore meet only two of the principal objections. In so doing, I shall attempt to elucidate what Anarchism really stands for.

The strange phenomenon of the opposition to Anarchism is that it brings to light the relation between so-called intelligence and ignorance. And yet this is not so very strange when we consider the relativity of all things. The ignorant mass has in its favor that it makes no pretense of knowledge or tolerance. Acting, as it always does, by mere impulse, its reasons are like those of a child. "Why?" "Because." Yet the opposition of the uneducated to Anarchism deserves the same consideration as that of the intelligent man.

What, then, are the objections? First, Anarchism is impractical, though a beautiful ideal. Second, Anarchism stands for violence and destruction, hence it must be repudiated as vile and dangerous. Both the intelligent man and the ignorant mass judge not from a thorough knowledge of the subject, but either from hearsay or false interpretation.

A practical scheme, says Oscar Wilde, is either one already in existence, or a scheme that could be carried out under the existing conditions; but it is exactly the existing conditions that one objects to, and any scheme that could accept these conditions is wrong and foolish. The true criterion of the practical, therefore, is not whether the latter can keep intact the wrong or foolish; rather it is whether the scheme has vitality enough to leave the stagnant waters of the old, and build, as well as sustain, new life. In the light of this conception, Anarchism is indeed practical. More than any other idea, it is helping to do away with the wrong and foolish; more than any other idea, it is building and sustaining new life.

The emotions of the ignorant man are continuously kept at a pitch by the most blood-curdling stories about Anarchism. Not a thing is too outrageous to be employed against this philosophy and its exponents. Therefore Anarchism represents to the unthinking what the proverbial bad man does to the child—a black monster bent on swallowing everything; in short, destruction and violence.

Destruction and violence! How is the ordinary man to know that the most violent element in society is ignorance; that its power of destruction is the very thing Anarchism is combating? Nor is he aware that Anarchism, whose roots, as it were, are part of nature's forces, destroys not healthful tissue, but parasitic growths that feed on the life's essence of society. It is merely clearing the soil from weeds and sagebrush, that it may eventually bear healthy fruit.

Someone has said that it requires less mental effort to condemn than to think. The widespread mental indolence, so prevalent in society, proves this to be only too true. Rather than to go to the bottom of any given idea, to examine into its origin and meaning, most people will either condemn it altogether, or rely on some superficial or prejudicial definition of non essentials.

Anarchism urges man to think, to investigate, to analyze every proposition; but that the brain capacity of the average reader be not taxed too much, I also shall begin with a definition, and then elaborate on the latter.

ANARCHISM: The philosophy of a new social order based on liberty unrestricted by man-made law; the theory that all forms of government rest on violence, and are therefore wrong and harmful, as well as unnecessary.

The new social order rests, of course, on the materialistic basis of life; but while all Anarchists agree that the main evil today is an economic one, they maintain that the solution of that evil can be brought about only through the consideration of *every phase* of life—individual, as well as the collective; the internal, as well as the external phases.

A thorough perusal of the history of human development will disclose two elements in bitter conflict with each other; elements that are only now beginning to be understood, not as foreign to each other, but as closely related and truly harmonious, if only placed in proper environment: the individual and social instincts. The individual and society have waged a relentless and bloody battle for ages, each striving for supremacy because each was blind to the value and importance of the other. The individual and social instincts—the one a most potent factor for individual endeavor, for growth, aspiration, self-realization; the other an equally potent factor for mutual helpfulness and social well-being.

The explanation of the storm raging within the individual, and between him and his surroundings, is not far to seek. The primitive man, unable to understand his being, much less the unity of all life, felt himself absolutely dependent on blind, hidden forces ever ready to mock and taunt him. Out of that attitude grew the religious concepts of man as a mere speck of dust dependent on superior powers on high, who can only be appeased by complete surrender. All the early sagas rest on that idea, which continues to be the *leitmotiv* of the biblical tales dealing with the relation of man to God, to the State, to society. Again and again the same motif, *man is nothing, the powers are everything.* Thus Jehovah would only endure man on condition of complete surrender. Man can have all the glories of the earth, but he must not become conscious of himself. The State, society, and moral laws all sing the same refrain: Man can have all the glories of the earth, but he must not become conscious of himself.

Anarchism is the only philosophy which brings to man the consciousness of himself; which maintains that God, the State, and society are nonexistent, that their promises are null and void, since they can be fulfilled only through man's subordination. Anarchism is therefore the teacher of the unity of life; not merely in nature, but in man. There is no conflict between the individual and the social instincts, any more than there is between the heart and the lungs: the one the receptacle of a precious life essence, the other the repository of the element that keeps the essence pure and strong. The individual is the heart of society, conserving the essence of social life; society is the lungs which are distributing the element to keep the life essence—that is, the individual—pure and strong.

"The one thing of value in the world," says Emerson, "is the active soul; this every man contains within him. The soul active sees absolute truth and utters truth and creates." In other words, the individual instinct is the thing of value in the world. It is the true soul that sees and creates the truth alive, out of which is to come a still greater truth, the reborn social soul.

Anarchism is the great liberator of man from the phantoms that have held him captive; it is the arbiter and pacifier of the two forces for individual and social harmony. To accomplish that unity, Anarchism has declared war on the pernicious influences which have so far prevented the harmonious blending of individual and social instincts, the individual and society.

Religion, the dominion of the human mind; Property, the dominion of human needs; and Government, the dominion of human conduct, represent the stronghold of man's enslavement and all the horrors it entails. Religion! How it dominates man's mind, how it humiliates and degrades his soul. God is everything, man is nothing, says religion. But out of that nothing God has created a kingdom so despotic, so tyrannical, so cruel, so terribly exacting that naught but gloom and tears and blood have ruled the world since gods began. Anarchism rouses man to rebellion against this black monster. Break your mental fetters, says Anarchism to man, for not until you think and judge for yourself will you get rid of the dominion of darkness, the greatest obstacle to all progress.

Property, the dominion of man's needs, the denial of the right to satisfy his needs. Time was when property claimed a divine right, when it came to man with the same refrain, even as religion, "Sacrifice! Abnegate! Submit!" The spirit of Anarchism has lifted man from his prostrate position. He now stands erect, with his face toward the light. He has learned to see the insatiable, devouring, devastating nature of property, and he is preparing to strike the monster dead.

"Property is robbery," said the great French Anarchist Proudhon. Yes, but without risk and danger to the robber. Monopolizing the accumulated efforts of man, property has robbed him of his birthright, and has turned him loose a pauper and an outcast. Property has not even the time-worn excuse that man does not create enough to satisfy all needs. The A B C student of economics knows that the productivity of labor within the last few decades far exceeds normal demand. But what are normal demands to an abnormal institution? The only demand that property recognizes is its own gluttonous appetite for greater wealth, because wealth means power; the power to subdue, to crush, to exploit; the power to enslave, to outrage, to degrade. America is particularly boastful of her great power, her enormous national wealth. Poor America, of what avail is all her wealth, if the individuals comprising the nation are wretchedly poor? If they live in squalor, in filth, in crime, with hope and joy gone, a homeless, soilless army of human prey.

It is generally conceded that unless the returns of any business venture exceed the cost, bankruptcy is inevitable. But those engaged in the business of producing wealth have not yet learned even this simple lesson. Every year the cost of production in human life is growing larger (50,000 killed, 100,000 wounded in America last year); the returns to the masses, who help to create wealth, are ever getting smaller. Yet America continues to be blind to the inevitable bankruptcy of our business of production. Nor is this the only crime of the latter. Still more fatal is the crime of turning the producer into a mere particle of a machine, with less will and decision than his master of steel and iron. Man is being robbed not merely of the products of his labor, but of the power of free initiative, of originality, and the interest in, or desire for, the things he is making.

Real wealth consists in things of utility and beauty, in things that help to create strong, beautiful bodies and surroundings inspiring to live in. But if man is doomed to wind cotton around a spool, or dig coal, or build roads for thirty years of his life, there can be no talk of wealth. What he gives to the world are only gray and hideous things, reflecting a dull and hideous existence—too weak to live, too cowardly to die. Strange to say, there are people who extol this deadening method of centralized production as the proudest achievement of our age. They fail utterly to realize that if we are to continue in machine subserviency, our slavery is more complete than was our bondage to the King. They do not want to know that centralization is not only the deathknell of liberty, but also of health and beauty, of art and science, all these being impossible in a clocklike, mechanical atmosphere.

Anarchism cannot but repudiate such a method of production: its goal is the freest possible expression of all the latent powers of the individual. Oscar Wilde defines a perfect personality as "one who develops under perfect conditions, who is not wounded, maimed, or in danger." A perfect personality, then, is only possible in a state of society where man is free to choose the mode of work, the conditions of work, and the freedom to work. One to whom the making of a table, the building of a house, or the tilling of the soil, is what the painting is to the artist and the discovery to the scientist—the result of inspiration, of intense longing, and deep interest in work as a creative force. That being the ideal of Anarchism, its economic arrangements must consist of voluntary productive and distributive associations, gradually developing into free communism, as the best means of producing with the least waste of human energy. Anarchism, however, also recognizes the right of the individual, or numbers of individuals, to arrange at all times for other forms of work, in harmony with their tastes and desires.

Such free display of human energy being possible only under complete individual and social freedom, Anarchism directs its forces against the third and greatest foe of all social equality; namely, the State, organized authority, or statutory law—the dominion of human conduct.

Just as religion has fettered the human mind, and as property, or the monopoly of things, has subdued and stifled man's needs, so has the State enslaved his spirit, dictating every phase of conduct. "All government in essence," says Emerson, "is tyranny." It matters not whether it is government by divine right or majority rule. In every instance its aim is the absolute subordination of the individual.

Referring to the American government, the greatest American Anarchist, David Thoreau, said: "Government, what is it but a tradition, though a recent one, endeavoring to transmit itself unimpaired to posterity, but each instance losing its integrity; it has not the vitality and force of a single living man. Law never made man a whit more just; and by means of their respect for it, even the well disposed are daily made agents of injustice."

Indeed, the keynote of government is injustice. With the arrogance and self-sufficiency of the King who could do no wrong, governments ordain, judge, condemn, and punish the most insignificant offenses, while maintaining themselves by the greatest of all offenses, the annihilation of individual liberty. Thus Ouida is right when she maintains that "the State only aims at instilling those qualities in its public by which its demands are obeyed, and its exchequer is filled. Its highest attainment is the reduction of mankind to clockwork. In its atmosphere all those finer and more delicate liberties, which require treatment and spacious expansion, inevitably dry up and perish. The State requires a taxpaying machine in which there is no hitch, an exchequer in which there is never a deficit, and a public, monotonous, obedient, colorless, spiritless, moving humbly like a flock of sheep along a straight high road between two walls."

Yet even a flock of sheep would resist the chicanery of the State, if it were not for the corruptive, tyrannical, and oppressive methods it employs to serve its purposes. Therefore Bakunin repudiates the State as synonymous with the surrender of the liberty of the individual or small minorities—the destruction of social relationship, the curtailment, or complete denial even, of life itself, for its own aggrandizement. The State is the altar of political freedom and, like the religious altar, it is maintained for the purpose of human sacrifice. . . .

. . . The political superstition is still holding sway over the hearts and minds of the masses, but the true lovers of liberty will have no more to do with it. Instead, they believe with Stirner that man has as much liberty as he is willing to take. Anarchism therefore stands for direct action, the open defiance of, and resistance to, all laws and restrictions, economic, social, and moral. But defiance and resistance are illegal. Therein lies the salvation of man. Everything illegal necessitates integrity, self-reliance, and courage. In short, it calls for free, independent spirits, for "men who are men, and who have a bone in their backs which you cannot pass your hand through."

Universal suffrage itself owes its existence to direct action. If not for the spirit of rebellion, of the defiance on the part of the American revolutionary fathers, their posterity would still wear the King's coat. If not for the direct action of a John Brown and his comrades, America would still trade in the flesh of the black man. True, the trade in white flesh is still going on; but that, too, will have to be abolished by direct action. Trade-unionism, the economic arena of the modern gladiator, owes its existence to direct action. It is but recently that law and government have attempted to crush the trade-union movement, and condemned the exponents of man's right to organize to prison as conspirators. Had they sought to assert their cause through begging, pleading, and compromise, trade-unionism would today be a negligible quantity. In France, in Spain, in Italy, in Russia, nay even in England (witness the growing rebellion of English labor unions), direct, revolutionary, economic action has become so strong a force in the battle for industrial liberty as to make the world realize the tremendous importance of labor's power. The General Strike, the supreme expression of the economic consciousness of the workers, was ridiculed in America but a short time ago. Today every great strike, in order to win, must realize the importance of the solidaric general protest.

Direct action, having proven effective along economic lines, is equally potent in the environment of the individual. There a hundred forces encroach upon his being, and only persistent resistance to them will finally set him free. Direct action against the authority in the shop, direct action against the authority of the law, direct action against the invasive, meddlesome authority of our moral code, is the logical, consistent method of Anarchism.

Will it not lead to a revolution? Indeed, it will. No real social change has ever come about without a revolution. People are either not familiar with their history, or they have not yet learned that revolution is but thought carried into action.

Anarchism, the great leaven of thought, is today permeating every phase of human endeavor. Science, art, literature, the drama, the effort for economic betterment, in fact every individual and social opposition to the existing disorder of things, is illumined by the spiritual light of Anarchism. It is the philosophy of the sovereignty of the individual. It is the theory of social harmony. It is the great, surging, living truth that is reconstructing the world, and that will usher in the Dawn.

3. CHARLOTTE PERKINS GILMAN

Herland
(1915)

CHARLOTTE PERKINS GILMAN (1860–1935) was a social critic, utopian novelist, and feminist-socialist whose trenchant analysis of the economic basis for women's subordination has had an enormous impact on modern feminism. After a tough childhood of abandonment, poverty, and inconsistent schooling, Gilman married Charles Stetson in 1884, gave birth to her only daughter, suffered a nervous breakdown (which she chronicled in her chilling 1892 short story "The Yellow Wall-Paper"), and finally divorced her husband in 1894 while she was living in Pasadena, California. A popular lecturer and prolific writer, Gilman earned widespread fame with the publication of *Woman and Economics* (1898), a pioneering work of sociology that examined sexual inequality as a function of women's economic dependence on men. Her most creative writing appeared between 1909 and 1916, when she served as editor of *The Forerunner*, a feminist magazine in which her witty and popular utopian novel, *Herland*, was serialized in 1915. *Herland* is a fictional tour through a futuristic utopian island community populated entirely by women and children, and governed by the principle of "New Motherhood," a cooperative feminist alternative to the male-dominated social-sexual order of late-nineteenth-century America. In the following chapter, "Comparisons Are Odious," the narrator and his male companions are humbled by the women they encounter in Herland. Gilman, however, never witnessed the feminist utopia she envisioned. She was diagnosed with inoperable breast cancer, and took her own life in 1935.

SOURCE: Charlotte Perkins Gilman. *Herland.* New York: Pantheon Books, 1979.

SELECTED READINGS: Joanne B. Karpinski, *Critical Essays on Charlotte Perkins Gilman* (1992). Mary A. Hill, *Charlotte Perkins Gilman: The Making of a Radical Feminist, 1860–1896* (1980). Ann J. Lane, *To Herland and Beyond: The Life and Work of Charlotte Perkins Gilman* (1980).

There you have it. You see, they were Mothers, not in our sense of helpless involuntary fecundity, forced to fill and overfill the land, every land, and then see their children suffer, sin, and die, fighting horribly with one another; but in the sense of Conscious Makers of People. Mother-love with them was not a brute passion, a mere "instinct," a wholly personal feeling; it was—a religion.

It included that limitless feeling of sisterhood, that wide unity in service which was so difficult for us to grasp. And it was National, Racial, Human—oh, I don't know how to say it.

We are used to seeing what we call "a mother" completely wrapped up in her own pink bundle of fascinating babyhood, and taking but the faintest theoretic interest in anybody else's bundle, to say nothing of the common needs of *all* the bundles. But these women were working all together at the grandest of tasks—they were Making People—and they made them well.

There followed a period of "negative eugenics" which must have been an appalling sacrifice. We are commonly willing to "lay down our lives" for our country, but they had to forego motherhood for their country—and it was precisely the hardest thing for them to do.

When I got this far in my reading I went to Somel for more light. We were as friendly by that time as I had ever been in my life with any woman. A mighty comfortable soul she was, giving one the nice smooth mother-feeling a man likes in a woman, and yet giving also the clear intelligence and dependableness I used to assume to be masculine qualities. We had talked volumes already.

"See here," said I. "Here was this dreadful period when they got far too thick, and decided to limit the population. We have a lot of talk about that among us, but your position is so different that I'd like to know a little more about it.

"I understand that you make Motherhood the highest social service—a sacrament, really; that it is only undertaken once, by the majority of the population; that those held unfit are not allowed even that; and that to be encouraged to bear more than one child is the very highest reward and honor in the power of the state."

(She interpolated here that the nearest approach to an aristocracy they had was to come of a line of "Over Mothers"—those who had been so honored.)

"But what I do not understand, naturally, is how you prevent it. I gathered that each woman had five. You have no tyrannical husbands to hold in check—and you surely do not destroy the unborn—"

The look of ghastly horror she gave me I shall never forget. She started from her chair, pale, her eyes blazing.

"Destroy the unborn—!" she said in a hard whisper. "Do men do that in your country?"

"Men!" I began to answer, rather hotly, and then saw the gulf before me. None of us wanted these women to think that *our* women, of whom we boasted so proudly, were in any way inferior to them. I am ashamed to say that I equivocated. I told her of certain criminal types of women—perverts, or crazy, who had been known to commit infanticide. I told her, truly enough, that there was much in our land which was open to criticism, but that I hated to dwell on our defects until they understood us and our conditions better.

And, making a wide detour, I scrambled back to my question of how they limited the population.

As for Somel, she seemed sorry, a little ashamed even, of her too clearly expressed amazement. As I look back now, knowing them better, I am more and more and more amazed as I appreciate the exquisite courtesy with which they had received over and over again statements and admissions on our part which must have revolted them to the soul.

She explained to me, with sweet seriousness, that as I had supposed, at first each woman bore five children; and that, in their eager desire to build up a nation, they had gone on in that way for a few centuries, till they were confronted with the absolute need of a limit. This fact was equally plain to all—all were equally interested.

They were now as anxious to check their wonderful power as they had been to develop it; and for some generations gave the matter their most earnest thought and study.

"We were living on rations before we worked it out," she said. "But we did work it out. You see, before a child comes to one of us there is a period of utter exaltation—the whole being is uplifted and filled with a concentrated desire for that child. We learned to look forward to that period with the greatest caution. Often our young women, those to whom motherhood had not yet come, would voluntarily defer it. When that deep inner demand for a child began to be felt she would deliberately engage in the most active work, physical and mental; and even more important, would solace her longing by the direct care and service of the babies we already had."

She paused. Her wise sweet face grew deeply, reverently tender.

"We soon grew to see that mother-love has more than one channel of expression. I think the reason our children are so—so fully loved, by all of us, is that we never—any of us—have enough of our own."

This seemed to me infinitely pathetic, and I said so. "We have much that is bitter and hard in our life at home," I told her, "but this seems to me piteous beyond words—a whole nation of starving mothers!"

But she smiled her deep contented smile, and said I quite misunderstood.

"We each go without a certain range of personal joy," she said, "but remember—we each have a million children to love and serve— *our* children."

It was beyond me. To hear a lot of women talk about "our children"! But I suppose that is the way the ants and bees would talk—do talk, maybe.

That was what they did, anyhow.

When a woman chose to be a mother, she allowed the child-longing to grow within her till it worked its natural miracle. When she did not so choose she put the whole thing out of her mind, and fed her heart with the other babies.

Let me see—with us, children—minors, that is—constitute about three-fifths of the population; with them only about one-third, or less. And precious—! No sole heir to an empire's throne, no solitary millionaire's baby, no only child of middle-aged parents, could compare as an idol with these Herland children.

But before I start on that subject I must finish up that little analysis I was trying to make.

They did effectually and permanently limit the population in numbers, so that the country furnished plenty for the fullest, richest life for all of them: plenty of everything, including room, air, solitude even.

And then they set to work to improve that population in quality—since they were restricted in quantity. This they had been at work on, uninterruptedly, for some fifteen hundred years. Do you wonder they were nice people?

Physiology, hygiene, sanitation, physical culture—all that line of work had been perfected long since. Sickness was almost wholly unknown among them, so much so that a previously high development in what we call the "science of medicine" had become practically a lost art. They were a clean-bred, vigorous lot, having the best of care, the most perfect living conditions always.

When it came to psychology—there was no one thing which left us so dumbfounded, so really awed, as the everyday working knowledge—and practice—they had in this line. As we learned more and more of it, we learned to appreciate the exquisite mastery with which we ourselves, strangers of alien race, of unknown opposite sex, had been understood and provided for from the first.

With this wide, deep, thorough knowledge, they had met and solved the problems of education in ways some of which I hope to make clear later. Those nation-loved children of theirs compared with the average in our country as the most perfectly cultivated, richly developed roses compare with—tumbleweeds. Yet they did not *seem* "cultivated" at all—it had all become a natural condition.

And this people, steadily developing in mental capacity, in will power, in social devotion, had been playing with the arts and sciences—as far as they knew them—for a good many centuries now with inevitable success.

Into this quiet lovely land, among these wise, sweet, strong women, we, in our easy assumption of superiority, had suddenly arrived; and now, tamed and trained to a degree they considered safe, we were at last brought out to see the country, to know the people.

4. EUGENE DEBS

Address to the Jury
(1918)

EUGENE DEBS's "Address to the Jury" was at once an indictment against government repression, a defense of free speech, and a celebration of the American radical tradition. Debs (1855–1926) was born in Terre Haute, Indiana, and he immersed himself in labor activity as a teen. In 1884 he was elected to the Indiana State Legislature as a Democrat. In that year he also participated in the famous Pullman Strike, which involved nearly one hundred thousand workers and briefly shut down the Western railroads; it ended in bloodshed after President Cleveland dispatched federal troops to Chicago. In 1898, Debs helped found the Socialist Democratic Party (renamed the Socialist Party in 1901), and he was a four-time presidential candidate. During World War I, Debs—a leading pacifist—made an antiwar speech in Canton, Ohio, in which he discouraged enlistment in the armed forces and encouraged insubordination in the military. This led to his indictment under the Espionage Act of 1917. Concluding his trial, Debs addressed the jury in his own defense. He was convicted and sentenced to a ten-year prison term. While still incarcerated in 1920, he gained nearly a million votes as the Socialist Party presidential candidate. Released in 1921 by President Harding, Debs continued to promote American socialism until his death in 1926.

SOURCE: Jean Y. Tussey, ed., *Eugene V. Debs Speaks.* New York: Pathfinder Press, 1970.

SELECTED READINGS: Eugene V. Debs, *Walls and Bars* (1927). Ray Ginger, *The Bending Cross: A Biography of Eugene Victor Debs* (1949). Nick Salvatore, *Eugene V. Debs: Citizen and Socialist* (1982).

May it please the court, and gentlemen of the jury:

When great changes occur in history, when great principles are involved, as a rule the majority are wrong. The minority are usually right. In every age there have been a few heroic souls who have been in advance of their time, who have been misunderstood, maligned, persecuted, sometimes put to death. Long after their martyrdom monuments were erected to them and garlands woven for their graves.

This has been the tragic history of the race. In the ancient world Socrates sought to teach some new truths to the people, and they made him drink the fatal hemlock. This has been true all along the track of the ages. The men and women who have been in advance, who have had new ideas, new ideals, who have had the courage to attack the established order of things, have all had to pay the same penalty.

A century and a half ago when the American colonists were still foreign subjects; when there were a few men who had faith in the common people and their destiny, and believed that they could rule themselves without a king; in that day to question the divine right of the king to rule was treason. If you will read Bancroft or any other American historian, you will find that a great majority of the colonists were loyal to the king and actually believed that he had a divine right to rule over them. . . . But there were a few men in that day who said, "We don't need a king; we can govern ourselves." And they began an agitation that has immortalized them in history.

Washington, Jefferson, Franklin, Paine and their compeers were the rebels of their day. When they began to chafe under the rule of a foreign king and to sow the seed of resistance among the colonists they were opposed by the people and denounced by the press. . . . But they had the moral courage to be true to their convictions, to stand erect and defy all the forces of reaction and detraction; and that is why their names shine in history, and why the great respectable majority of their day sleep in forgotten graves.

At a later time there began another mighty agitation in this country. It was directed against an institution that was deemed eminently respectable in its time—the age-old, cruel and infamous institution of chattel slavery. . . . All the organized forces of society and all the powers of government upheld and defended chattel slavery in that day. And again the few advanced thinkers, crusaders and martyrs appeared. One of the first was Elijah Lovejoy who was murdered in cold blood at Alton, Illinois, in 1837 because he was opposed to chattel slavery—just as I am opposed to wage slavery. Today as you go up or down the Mississippi River and look up at the green hills at Alton, you see a magnificent white shaft erected there in memory of the man who was true to himself and his convictions of right and duty even unto death.

It was my good fortune to personally know Wendell Phillips. I heard the story of his cruel and cowardly persecution from his own eloquent lips just a little while before they were silenced in death.

William Lloyd Garrison, Wendell Phillips, Elizabeth Cady Stanton, Susan B. Anthony, Gerrit Smith, Thaddeus Stevens and other leaders of the abolition movement who were regarded as public enemies and treated accordingly, were true to their faith and stood their ground. They are all in history. You are now teaching your children to revere their memories, while all of their detractors are in oblivion.

Chattel slavery has disappeared. But we are not yet free. We are engaged today in another mighty agitation. It is as wide as the world. It means the rise of the toiling masses who are gradually becoming conscious of their interests, their power, and their mission as a class; who are organizing industrially and politically and who are slowly but surely developing the economic and political power that is to set them free. These awakening workers are still in a minority, but they have learned how to work together to achieve their freedom, and how to be patient and abide their time.

From the beginning of the war to this day I have never by word or act been guilty of the charges embraced in this indictment. If I have criticized, if I have condemned, it is because I believed it to be my duty, and that it was my right to do so under the laws of the land. I have had ample precedents for my attitude. This country has been engaged in a number of wars and every one of them has been condemned by some of the people, among them some of the most eminent men of their time. The war of the American Revolution was violently opposed. The Tory press representing the "upper classes" denounced its leaders as criminals and outlaws.

The war of 1812 was opposed and condemned by some of the most influential citizens; the Mexican war was vehemently opposed and bitterly denounced, even after the war had been declared and was in progress, by Abraham Lincoln, Charles Sumner, Daniel Webster, Henry Clay and many other well-known and influential citizens. These men denounced the President, they condemned his administration while the war was being waged, and they charged in substance that the war was a crime against humanity. They were not indicted; they were not charged with treason nor tried for crime. They are honored today by all of their countrymen.

The Civil War between the states met with violent resistance and passionate condemnation. In the year 1864 the Democratic Party met in national convention at Chicago and passed a resolution condemning the war as a failure. What would you say if the Socialist Party were to meet in convention today and condemn the present war as a failure? You charge us with being disloyalists and traitors. Were the Democrats of 1864 disloyalists and traitors because they condemned the war as a failure?

And if so, why were they not indicted and prosecuted accordingly? I believe in the Constitution. Isn't it strange that we Socialists stand almost alone today in upholding and defending the Constitution of the United States? The revolutionary fathers who had been oppressed under king rule understood that free speech, a free press and the right of free assemblage by the people were fundamental principles in democratic government. The very first amendment to the Constitution reads:

> "Congress shall make no law respecting an establishment of religion, or prohibiting the free exercise thereof; or abridging the freedom of speech, or of the press; or the right of the people peaceably to assemble, and to petition the government for a redress of grievances."

That is perfectly plain English. It can be understood by a child. I believe the revolutionary fathers meant just what is here stated—that Congress shall make no law abridging the freedom of speech or of the press, or of the right of the people to peaceably assemble, and to petition the government for a redress of their grievances.

That is the right I exercised at Canton on the sixteenth day of last June; and for the exercise of that right, I now have to answer to this indictment. I believe in the right of free speech, in war as well as in peace. I would not, under any circumstances, suppress free speech. It is far more dangerous to attempt to gag the people than to allow them to speak freely what is in their hearts.

I have told you that I am no lawyer, but it seems to me that I know enough to know that if Congress enacts any law that conflicts with this provision in the Constitution, that law is void. If the Espionage Law finally stands, then the Constitution of the United States is dead. If that law is not the negation of every fundamental principle established by the Constitution, then certainly I am unable to read or to understand the English language. . . .

Now, gentlemen of the jury, I am not going to detain you too long. . . . I cannot take back a word I have said. I cannot repudiate a sentence I have uttered. I stand before you guilty of having made this speech. . . . I do not know, I cannot tell, what your verdict may be; nor does it matter much, so far as I am concerned.

Gentlemen, I am the smallest part of this trial. I have lived long enough to realize my own personal insignificance in relation to a great issue that involves the welfare of the whole people. What you may choose to do to me will be of small consequence after all. I am not on trial here. There is an infinitely greater issue that is being tried today in this court, though you may not be conscious of it. American institutions are on trial here before a court of American citizens. The future will render the final verdict.

And now, your honor, permit me to return my thanks for your patient consideration. And to you, gentlemen of the jury, for the kindness with which you have listened to me.

I am prepared for your verdict.

5. MARCUS GARVEY

Africa for the Africans
(1923)

In **"Africa for the Africans,"** MARCUS GARVEY championed the twin goals of race pride and race solidarity. Garvey (1887–1940) was born in Jamaica, and in 1914 he founded the Universal Negro Improvement Association (UNIA) for the "general uplift of the Negro peoples of the world." Garvey arrived in Harlem in 1916, and by the early 1920s the UNIA had become the largest black activist organization in American history. However, Garvey clashed with other African-American leaders (most notoriously, with W. E. B. Du Bois), and the UNIA weakened in the face of government repression as well as Garvey's own mismanagement. In 1925, Garvey was convicted of mail fraud and he spent three years in prison before being deported to Jamaica in 1927. "Africa for the Africans" promoted Garvey's vision of a great black empire in Africa.

SOURCE: Marcus Garvey. *Philosophy and Opinions of Marcus Garvey.* Amy Jacques-Garvey, ed. New York: Atheneum, 1925.

SELECTED READINGS: Tony Martin, *Race First: The Ideological and Organizational Struggles of Marcus Garvey and the Universal Negro Improvement Association* (1976). Theodore G. Vincent, *Black Power and the Garvey Movement* (1971). Edmund David Cronon, *Black Moses: The Story of Marcus Garvey and the Universal Negro Improvement Association* (1955).

For five years the Universal Negro Improvement Association has been advocating the cause of Africa for the Africans—that is, that the Negro peoples of the world should concentrate upon the object of building up for themselves a great nation in Africa.

When we started our propaganda toward this end several of the so-called intellectual Negroes who have been bamboozling the race for over half a century said that we were crazy, that the Negro peoples of the western world were not interested in Africa and could not live in Africa. One editor and leader went so far as to say at his so-called Pan-African Congress that American Negroes could not live in Africa, because the climate was too hot. All kinds of arguments have been adduced by these Negro intellectuals against the colonization of Africa by the black race. Some said that the black man would ultimately work out his existence alongside of the white man in countries founded and established by the latter. Therefore, it was not necessary for Negroes to seek an independent nationality of their own. The old time stories of "African fever," "African bad climate," "African mosquitoes," "African savages," have been repeated by these "brainless intellectuals" of ours as a scare against our people in America and the West Indies taking a kindly interest in the new program of building a racial empire of our own in our Motherland. Now that years have rolled by and the Universal Negro Improvement Association has made the circuit of the world with its propaganda, we find eminent statesmen and leaders of the white race coming out boldly advocating the cause of colonizing Africa with the Negroes of the western world. A year ago Senator MacCullum of the Mississippi Legislature introduced a resolution in the House for the purpose of petitioning the Congress of the United States of America and the President to use their good influence in securing from the Allies sufficient territory in Africa in liquidation of the war debt, which territory should be used for the establishing of an independent nation for American Negroes. About the same time Senator France of Maryland gave expression to a similar desire in the Senate of the United States. During a speech on the "Soldiers' Bonus," he said: "We owe a big debt to Africa and one which we have too long ignored. I need not enlarge upon our peculiar interest in the obligation to the people of Africa.

Thousands of Americans have for years been contributing to the missionary work which has been carried out by the noble men and women who have been sent out in that field by the churches of America."

The Dream of a Negro Empire

It is only a question of a few more years when Africa will be completely colonized by Negroes, as Europe is by the white race. What we want is an independent African nationality, and if America is to help the Negro peoples of the world establish such a nationality, then we welcome the assistance.

It is hoped that when the time comes for American and West Indian Negroes to settle in Africa, they will realize their responsibility and their duty. It will not be to go to Africa for the purpose of exercising an over-lordship over the natives, but it shall be the purpose of the Universal Negro Improvement Association to have established in Africa that brotherly co-operation which will make the interests of the African native and the American and West Indian Negro one and the same; that is to say, we shall enter into a common partnership to build up Africa in the interests of our race.

Oneness of Interests

Everybody knows that there is absolutely no difference between the native African and the American and West Indian Negroes, in that we are descendants from one common family stock. It is only a matter of accident that we have been divided and kept apart for over three hundred years, but it is felt that when the time has come for us to get back together, we shall do so in the spirit of brotherly love, and any Negro who expects that he will be assisted here, there or anywhere by the Universal Negro Improvement Association to exercise a haughty superiority over the fellows of his own race, makes a tremendous mistake. Such men had better remain where they are and not attempt to become in any way interested in the higher development of Africa.

The Negro has had enough of the vaunted practice of race superiority as inflicted upon him by others, therefore he is not prepared to tolerate a similar assumption on the part of his own people. In America and the West Indies, we have Negroes who believe themselves so much above their fellows as to cause them to think that any readjustment in the affairs of the race should be placed in their hands for them to exercise a kind of an autocratic and despotic control as others have done to us for centuries. Again I say, it would be advisable for such Negroes to take their hands and minds off the now popular idea of colonizing Africa in the interest of the Negro race, because their being identified with this new program will not in any way help us, because of the existing feeling among Negroes everywhere not to tolerate the infliction of race or class superiority upon them, as is the desire of the self-appointed and self-created race leadership that we have been having for the last fifty years.

The Basis of an African Aristocracy

The masses of Negroes in America, the West Indies, South and Central America are in sympathetic accord with the aspirations of the native Africans. We desire to help them build up Africa as a Negro Empire, where every black man, whether he was born in Africa or in the Western world, will have the opportunity to develop on his own lines under the protection of the most favorable democratic institutions.

It will be useless, as before stated, for bombastic Negroes to leave America and the West Indies to go to Africa, thinking that they will have privileged positions to inflict upon the race that bastard aristocracy that they have tried to maintain in this Western world at the expense of the masses. Africa shall develop an aristocracy of its own, but it shall be based upon service and loyalty to race. Let all Negroes work toward that end. I feel that it is only a question of a few more years before our program will be accepted not only by the few statesmen of America who are now interested in it, but by the strong statesmen of the world, as the only solution to the great race problem. There is no other way to avoid the threatening war of the races that is bound to engulf all mankind, which has been prophesied by the world's greatest thinkers; there is no better method than by apportioning every race to its own habitat.

The time has really come for the Asiatics to govern themselves in Asia, as the Europeans are in Europe and the Western world; so also is it wise for the Africans to govern themselves at home, and thereby bring peace and satisfaction to the entire human family.

6. HUEY LONG

Share Our Wealth

(1935)

One of the most controversial figures in modern American political history, **HUEY LONG**'s response to the Great Depression was the Share Our Wealth movement. Born on a farm near Winnfield, Louisiana, Long (1893–1935) worked as a traveling salesman before attending (and dropping out of) Tulane Law School. Nevertheless, he passed the state bar exam in 1915 at age twenty-one. A man of great energy and ambition, Long was elected governor of Louisiana in 1928. Although he put thousands to work on public projects, paved thousands of miles of roads, and distributed free textbooks to schoolchildren, Long was also a ruthless and corrupt politician who sometimes resorted to demagoguery. He became a U.S. senator in 1930, where he frequently drew the ire of business interests as well as the Roosevelt Administration, which was threatened by his popularity. Long believed that concentrated wealth was one of the greatest dangers facing society, and he claimed that as many as 7.5 million citizens joined the Share Our Wealth clubs that he helped form in 1934. Long planned to run for president but was assassinated in 1935; Robert Penn Warren's fictionalized account of Long's life, *All the King's Men*, won the Pulitzer Prize in 1946.

SOURCE: Huey Long, "To Members and Well-Wishers of the Share Our Wealth Society," *Congressional Record*, 74th U.S. Congress, 1st Session, Vol. 79. Washington, D.C.: U.S. Government Printing Office, 1935;

reprinted in Henry C. Dethloff, ed., *Huey P. Long: Southern Demagogue or American Democrat?* Lafayette: University of Southwestern Louisiana Press, 1976.

SELECTED READINGS: Alan Brinkley, *Voices of Protest: Huey Long, Father Coughlin, and the Great Depression* (1982). Robert Penn Warren, *All the King's Men* (1960). T. Harry Williams, *Huey Long* (1981).

To Members and Well-Wishers of the Share Our Wealth Society: For twenty years I have been in the battle to provide that, so long as America has, or can produce, an abundance of the things which make life comfortable and happy, that none should own so much of the things which he does not need and cannot use, as to deprive the balance of the people of a reasonable proportion of the necessities and conveniences of life. The whole line of my political thought has always been that America must face the time when the whole country would shoulder the obligation which it owes to every child born on earth,—that is, a fair chance to life, liberty, and happiness. . . .

Here is the whole sum and substance of the Share Our Wealth movement:

1. Every family[is] to be furnished by the government a homestead allowance, free of debt, of not less than one-third the average family wealth of the country, which means, at the lowest, that every family shall have the reasonable comforts of life up to a value of from $5,000 to $6,000: No person to have a fortune of more than 100 to 300 times the average family fortune, which means that the limit to fortune is between $1,500,000 and $5,000,000, with annual capital levy taxes imposed on all above $1,000,000.

2. The yearly income of every family shall be not less than one-third of the average family income, which means that, according to the estimates of the statisticians of the U.S. Government and Wall Street, no family's annual income would be less than from $2,000 to $2,500: No yearly income shall be allowed to any person larger than from 100 to 300 times the size of the average family income, which means that no person would be allowed to earn in any year more than from $600,000 to $1,800,000, all to be subject to present income tax laws.

3. To limit or regulate the hours of work to such an extent as to prevent over-production; the most modern and efficient machinery would be encouraged so that as much would be produced as possible so as to satisfy all demands of the people, but to also allow the maximum time to the workers for recreation, convenience, education, and luxuries of life.

4. An old age pension to the persons over 60.

5. To balance agricultural production with what can be consumed according to the laws of God, which includes the preserving and storing of surplus commodities to be paid for and held by the Government for the emergencies when such are needed. Please bear in mind, however, that when the people of America have had money to buy things they needed, we have never had a surplus of any commodity. This plan of God does not call for destroying any of the things raised to eat or wear, nor does it countenance whole destruction of hogs, cattle or milk.

6. To pay the veterans of our wars what we owe them and to care for their disabled.

7. Education and training for all children to be equal in opportunity in all schools, colleges, universities and other institutions for training in the professions and vocations of life; to be regulated on the capacity of children to learn, and not on the ability of parents to pay the costs. Training for life's work to be as much universal and thorough for all walks in life as has been the training in the arts of killing.

8. The raising of revenue and taxes for the support of this program to come from the reduction of swollen fortunes from the top, as well as for the support of public works to give employment whenever there may be any slackening necessary in private enterprise.

I now ask those who read this circular to help us at once in this work of giving life and happiness to our people,—not a starvation dole upon which someone may live in misery from week to week. Before this miserable system of wreckage has destroyed the life germ of respect and culture in our American people, let us save what was here, merely by having none too poor and none too rich. The theory of the Share Our Wealth Society is to have enough for all, but not to have one with so much that less than enough remains for the balance of the people.

Please, therefore, let me ask you who read this document,—please help this work before it is too late for us to be of help to our people. We ask you now, (1) help to get your neighbor into the work of this Society, and (2) help get other Share Our Wealth societies started in your county and in adjoining counties and get them to go out to organize other societies.

To print and mail out this circular costs about 60¢ per hundred, or $6.00 per thousand. Anyone who reads this who wants more circulars of this kind to use in the work, can get them for that price by sending the money to me, and I will pay the printer for him. Better still, if you can, have this circular reprinted in your own town or city.

Let everyone who feels he wishes to help in our work start right out and go ahead. One man or woman is as important as any other. Take up the fight! Do not wait for someone else to tell you what to do. There are no high lights in this effort. We have no state managers and no city managers. Everyone can take up the work and as many societies can be organized as there are people to organize them. One is the same as another. The reward and compensation is the salvation of humanity. Fear no opposition. "He who falls in this fight falls in the radiance of the future!"

Yours sincerely,
Huey P. Long,
United States Senator,
Washington, D. C.

7. PAUL ROBESON

My Answer

(1949)

PAUL LEROY ROBESON (1898–1976) was a supremely talented African-American entertainer and political activist. He was born in Princeton, New Jersey, and he graduated at the top of his class from Rutgers University in 1919, where he was also an All-American running back. Then he attended Columbia Law School and briefly became a lawyer, before pursuing his real loves of singing and acting in the early 1920s. In 1930 he earned his reputation as one of the great Shakespearian actors when he played the part of the Moor in *Othello*. However, he also encountered a great deal of racism during his career as a performer, and soon he began immersing himself in political activism. In the 1940s he became notorious as a result of his statements in favor of the Soviet Union, which he believed was superior to the United States in many respects. In retaliation, the U.S. government denied him a passport to travel abroad, thereby helping to ruin his career. In the remarks below, Robeson defended his controversial beliefs in favor of black equality, black cultural nationalism, and an end to colonialism in Africa.

SOURCE: Paul Robeson, "My Answer," as told to Dan Burley, *New York Age* (August 6, 13, 20 and September 3, 17, 1949), reprinted in Philip S. Foner, ed., *Paul Robeson Speaks: Writings, Speeches, Interviews, 1918–1974*.

SELECTED READINGS: Martin B. Duberman, *Paul Robeson* (2005). Paul Robeson, *Here I Stand* (1988).

I'm in the headlines and they're saying all manner of things about me such as "enemy" of the land of my birth, "traitor" to my country, "dangerous radical" and that I am an "ungrateful" cur. But they can't say that I am not 100 per cent for my people. The American Press has set out on its own campaign of deliberate misquotation and distortion of the things I say and do, trying to set my people against me, but they can't win because what I say is the unadulterated truth which cannot be denied.

Everybody is trying to explain Paul Robeson. That isn't hard. I'm just an ordinary guy like anyone else, trying to do what I can to make things match, to find and tie up the loose ends. I am asked, do I think the salvation of the American Negro lies in complete integration—social, political and economic, or in a highly developed Negro nationalism. Let me answer it in my way.

The whole Negro problem has its basis in the South—in the cotton belt where Negroes are in the majority. That is the only thing that explains me completely. The Negro upper class wants to know why I am out here struggling in behalf of the oppressed, exploited Negro of the South when I could isolate myself from them like they do and become wealthy by keeping quiet on such disturbing subjects. This, I have found, would not be true of me. What I earn doesn't help my people that much. I have relatives in the South still struggling to make a living. The other night in Newark, one relative of mine was in the audience. He is a mason and a carpenter. What I do personally doesn't help him. I found I have to think of the whole background of the Negro problem. Therefore I have taken my obligations to the Negro people very seriously.

I have asked myself, just what Negro people am I fighting for? The big Negroes take it that I am fighting for them and since they're comfortable and living good, they don't want too much fighting or things said that might prove embarrassing to their positions. My travels abroad, however, have shown me what and whom I am fighting for. During my travels, I met native Africans, West Indians, Chinese,

East Indians and other dark people who are fighting for the same thing—freedom from bondage of the imperialistic Wall St., the bankers and the plantation bosses, whether in London or in New York. The big Negro wants somebody to fight for him, but his objectives are purely selfish. If I am fighting for the Negroes on Strivers Row, I must fight for every Negro, wherever he may be.

Let's return again to the fact that the whole Negro problem has its basis in the South. Do you know that out of 15 million Negroes in the United States, nearly 10 million live and die in the South? I've got to be interested in basic problems, the people and conditions on the lower levels of life. I found that Negroes constitute 98 per cent of the population of the West Indies. Without the Negro there could be no economic South and there could be no economic West Indies to make the bankers and overlords of Wall St. fabulously wealthy. In the South, Negroes do most of the work and get nothing from it in return.

I understand these things better on my travels abroad. In England I met boys and girls from Africa working on ships, in the schools and elsewhere and I met fellows from the West Indian Islands, all trying to work out their destinies the best way they could. It became very clear to me what is happening to them. The continent of Africa belongs to them and should belong to them now. The same goes for the West Indies which the Negro built up, only to have a few people from the United States and from England move in and take it away from them and then rule them by absentee landlordism with headquarters in Wall St. and in London. These are the people who own the sugar plantations in the West Indies and in Louisiana and the tobacco plantations in North Carolina.

It is very easy to see, as in the question of India, China, Africa and the West Indies, the future of these people in the independence of their own countries. I see the Negro's struggle as demanding great concentration on the question as to where he is going and who is leading him there. We must come together as a people, unite and close ranks and with our own unity we must try and find the right allies— those whose struggles are identical to our own. We cannot escape the fact that our struggles over the last 300 years have driven us together.

Suppose that in the South, where the Negroes are in the majority in the agricultural belt, we had the vote like everyone else. What would happen? Wouldn't Negroes be in Congress, be governors, judges, mayors, sheriffs and so on? Wouldn't they be in control in the South and run things as the minority people down there are doing at this very moment?

There you have your answer to that charge that I am fomenting strife and plotting with a foreign government to establish a Black Republic in the South. What would happen—even tomorrow—if the Negro was allowed to vote? Without any nonsense, you would have a tremendous concentration of Negro power in the United States. Many people would object and oppose it on various grounds, principally racial and economic, but you have a concentration of Irish power in Boston, Italian power in New York, and so on. Nobody has made a major issue of that, have they? What is wrong with our struggle for our right to vote, for economic liberation, for civil rights? To me, from the economic point of view, we should think of spreading our strength around so as not to put all our wealth and power into the hands of a few Negroes who would exploit that power like any reactionary banker to the detriment of Negroes in the United States.

There are two groups of people who are worried stiff about the growth of the unified power of the Negro people: one group includes the Dixiecrats like Rankin of Mississippi, Wood and George of Georgia, Tom Connally of Texas and Eastland of Mississippi. The other includes the reactionary industrialists and financiers who own many of the farms and plantations in the South on which my people and your people are enslaved right now. These are the people who work to keep the Negro in bondage.

My basic point is that these are the fellows who want the Negro to be loyal to them, to die for them in war, to make a profit for them.

We Negroes must think this thing out. What America are we fighting for? Obviously we don't live alone in America, so we must choose the right allies, as I said before, and these allies cannot be those Dixiecrats as named here. They cannot be those bankers and international financiers who run most of the country and own today all the resources of the South built on the labor of the Negro people. They own the sugar, the tobacco, the mineral wealth. They own the West Indies where Negroes are 98 per cent of the population.

They are the ones who helped take Africa from the African people. Our allies must be the progressive section of the American people— the honest progressives who find kinship in the common struggle for freedom, equality and unity. And who are these progressives? They are those who swell the ranks of labor: the poor white sharecropper of the South, presently being used as a tool by the rich plantation owners and bankers to pull their chestnuts out of the fire by warring on their Negro neighbors; the small business man and others of all races, colors, creeds and national origins, including the small, independent farmer—people who are passed up when the profits are handed out but who are the first thrown into the pot to cook up those profits for someone else. The Dixiecrats, like Wood of Georgia and those powerful reactionaries who hope to stamp out the militant struggle of the Negro for complete freedom, equality and civil rights, hope to keep all the wealth for themselves.

They are the ones who are behind the House Un-American Committee. They are the ones ceaselessly pushing the persecution of those unafraid to speak out and to champion the man down under, whether he be black or white.

When some of our leading Negroes select those most guilty of exploiting their people to get thick with in their social and economic affairs, they pick the wrong people no matter what excuse might be presented. Leopards don't change their spots and neither do those who think about us adversely change their thoughts overnight. This sort of thing I'd call "20th Century Uncle Tommism"—going back to the Big House to fawn at the boss' feet—and we shouldn't tolerate it one minute if we expect to get ahead.

Me? I'm out with the field hand. That's the only way I can see it. They tell us to stay in our place. Well, I'm staying in mine—out here with the field hand—the little fellow, the guy who gets pushed around, the fellow who has to do all the hard work and gets nothing from it.

I'm talking about the sharecroppers, Negro and white, on the sprawling plantations in the South.

I'm talking about the tobacco, steel and lumber workers; the men who tote the sandbags with chains about their legs to stem the Mississippi at flood time so as to save the empire of some guy in New York, London or Paris who has never seen the land which keeps him in luxury nor met and talked with the people on whose backs his kingdom rests.

Yes, that's the only way I can see it—stay with, work with, fight with and sing with the field hand, and if we stick it out long enough—we'll get the Big House!

We must solve our problem where we find it. Not by going thousands of miles away to take up something we are not familiar with.

Why should we leave the United States without first getting what is coming to us through a militant struggle to gain the profits that have come from our labor, our blood, our sweat, our tears? I'm talking now about the various schemes that would arouse false hopes in the Negro people about taking some other land as a homeland when we already have our home right here on American soil which will be ours when we make it our own.

Think what a Federation of the West Indies would mean economically. With Negroes 98 per cent of the West Indian population, why shouldn't they control the sugar, tourist trade, the banana and rum industries and the possibilities of further industrial development of the islands? Think of the amount of base metals and the other natural wealth to be found there.

A Federation of the West Indies would give Negroes a completely integrated economy that would make the West Indies one of the most important places in the world—connected with the Latin and South American mainland. Think of the strategic position a native West Indian–controlled political and economic federation would command. Think of the weight such a setup would throw in United Nations circles.

Suppose Africa were free and a great nation like China. We have to think for ourselves and also to include in intelligent thought those who are closest to us through the ties of blood, nationality, common interest and mutual aspirations. We want as many areas in this changing world of control as we can get as Negro people. Suppose we won the right to vote plus our proper share of the economic spoils of the South: think of the tremendous pressure Negroes could bring upon the United Nations to help kindred people in other parts of the world. There is no reason to change what have become very significant and historic facts. Certainly, any Negro in the world would have a deep feeling for his own people, wherever they are, whatever conditions they might be in.

As chairman of the Council on African Affairs, I can truthfully say that the African people are highly cultured and not savage and cannibalistic as the newspaper, radio, book and lecture propagandists would make them. That is the Dixiecrat program to keep us fighting one another and to lead us away from the true paths that lead to the doorway to freedom from which we have been detoured over the centuries.

I am proud of my African heritage. In fact, I'm so proud of it that I have made it my work to learn several African languages for conversation and musical purposes. Mrs. Robeson has been in South Africa, in the Uganda and in the Belgian Congo and the French Cameroons. She has written a book on Africa, *African Journey*. I expect to be in Nigeria and French West Africa next year. There is a tremendous liberation movement now under way in Nigeria of which Azikiwe is the brilliant, capable and resourceful leader. It is very possible that Nigeria will be the first African nation to win complete liberation. Understand that we over here, whether from the West Indies or from New York, should consult with the Africans about taking something from them. This is in answer to the question: What Do You Think of the Back-to-Africa Movement?

At the Paris Peace Conference which brought all the reactionaries of America down on my neck, a Negro from French Africa spoke for an organization of one million Africans formed into trade unions in West Africa. In East Africa, Uganda and Kenya, there are very powerful movements for the rights of the African peoples. We must be very much aware of our allies of this time—and here we are dealing with 150 million in Africa, 40 to 60 million in the Caribbean and Latin America. All these people are to be considered, to be thought of as strengthening their own position in the areas where they live.

Likewise Negroes in the South and West Indies must think of the areas in which they live as land that belongs to them. That is where they worked or were worked to build up things—to till the soil, plant and harvest; to chop down trees and milk them of turpentine and other basic products for the industrial mills of the imperialists and warmongers.

They—the Negroes of the South—must not grow to thank John Rankin for being allowed to live down there. They must realize that they are the ones who built that which has been and still is being taken from them. Maybe, they should think of someday gaining control through constitutional means of that which should have been theirs all along.

Where will the next Peekskill be? What new battle ground have the reactionary police and those behind them selected? Where will they demonstrate further the "old Southern Custom" of beating in the heads of Negroes and all those identified with the struggle to free the Negro people? I mean completely free the Negro from the shackles of the greedy exploiters of his labor and his talents. To be completely free from the chains that bind him, the Negro must be part of the progressive forces which are fighting the overall battle of the little guy—the sharecropper, the drugstore clerk, the auto mechanic, the porter and the maid, the owner of the corner diner, the truck driver, the garment, mill and steel workers. The progressive section sees no color line and views the whole problem of race and color prejudices and discrimination as a divisional tactic of those busy pitting class against class, dividing the masses into tiny, warring factions that produces nothing for them but discord and misery while a scant, privileged few takes all the wealth, holds the power and dictates the terms. This concentration of power in the hands of less than a hundred men is so strong that it can decide who shall eat and who shall not, who shall have decent homes and who shall be doomed to crowded tenements that are firetraps and rat-infested holes where children must be reared and the occupants live and die in despair.

I am well equipped now, although I have not always been so, to make the supreme fight for my people and all the other underprivileged masses wherever they may be. Here, I speak of those bereft of uncompromising, courageous leadership that cannot be bought, cannot be intimidated, and cannot be swerved from its purpose of bringing true freedom to those who follow it. God gave me the voice that people want to hear, whether in song or in speech. I shall take my voice wherever there are those who want to hear the melody of freedom or the words that might inspire hope and courage in the face of despair and fear.

I told the American Legion that I have been to Memphis, Tennessee, the stamping grounds of such Negro-haters as Ed Crump and others of the cracker breed, and I have been to the lynch belt of Florida. I told the Legion I would return to Peekskill. I did. I will go North, South, East or West, Europe, Africa, South America, Asia or Australia and fight for the freedom of the people. This thing burns in me and it is not my nature nor inclination to be scared off.

They revile me, scandalize me, and try to holler me down on all sides. That's all right. It's okay. Let them continue. My voice topped the blare of the Legion bands and the hoots of the hired hoodlums who attempted to break up my concert appearance for the Harlem Division of the Civil Rights Congress. It will be heard above the screams of the intolerant, the jeers of the ignorant pawns of the small groups of the lousy rich who would drown out the voice of a champion of the underdog. My weapons are peaceful for it is only by peace that peace can be attained. Their weapons are the nightsticks of the fascist police, the bloodhounds of the cracker sheriffs in the backwoods of the South, the trained voices of the choirs of hate. The song of freedom must prevail.

8. JO ANN ROBINSON

The Montgomery Bus Boycott
and the Women Who Made It
(1955)

JO ANN ROBINSON's account of the Montgomery Bus Boycott of 1955–1956 draws attention to the wide-ranging, grassroots nature of that protest. Robinson (1912–1992) was a professor at Alabama State College and president of the Women's Political Council (WPC) of Montgomery, Alabama, when Rosa Parks broke a segregation ordinance by famously refusing to give up her seat on a local bus. In response, Robinson and other members of the WPC helped organize and sustain a yearlong boycott of Montgomery's city buses. By the time the boycott was over, local buses were desegregated, Martin Luther King, Jr., had emerged as a national leader, and the modern civil rights movement was underway.

SOURCE: Jo Ann Robinson. *The Montgomery Bus Boycott and the Women Who Made It: The Memoir of Jo Ann Gibson Robinson.* Edited with a foreword by David J. Garrow. Knoxville: University of Tennessee Press, 1987.

SELECTED READINGS: Brian Ward and Tony Badger, *The Making of Martin Luther King and the Civil Rights Movement* (1996). Vicki I. Crawford, Jacqueline Anne Rouse, and Burton Woods, *Women in the Civil Rights Movement, 1941–1965* (1990). Martin Luther King, Jr., *Stride Toward Freedom: The Montgomery Story* (1958).

In October 1955, Mary Louise Smith, an eighteen-year-old black girl, was arrested and fined for refusing to move to the rear of the bus. Her case was unpublicized and no one knew about it until after her arrest and conviction. She, too, was found guilty; she paid her fine and kept on riding the bus.

In the afternoon of Thursday, December 1, a prominent black woman named Mrs. Rosa Parks was arrested for refusing to vacate her seat for a white man. Mrs. Parks was a medium-sized, cultured mulatto woman; a civic and religious worker; quiet, unassuming, and pleasant in manner and appearance; dignified and reserved; of high morals and a strong character. She was—and still is, for she lives to tell the story—respected in all black circles. By trade she was a seamstress, adept and competent in her work.

Tired from work, Mrs. Parks boarded a bus. The "reserved seats" were partially filled, but the seats just behind the reserved section were vacant, and Mrs. Parks sat down in one. It was during the busy evening rush hour. More black and white passengers boarded the bus, and soon all the reserved seats were occupied. The driver demanded that Mrs. Parks get up and surrender her seat to a white man, but she was tired from her work. Besides, she was a woman, and the person waiting was a man. She remained seated. In a few minutes, police summoned by the driver appeared, placed Mrs. Parks under arrest, and took her to jail.

It was the first time the soft-spoken, middle-aged woman had been arrested. She maintained decorum and poise, and the word of her arrest spread. Mr. E. D. Nixon, a longtime stalwart of our NAACP branch, along with liberal white attorney Clifford Durr and his wife Virginia, went to jail and obtained Mrs. Parks's release on bond. Her trial was scheduled for Monday, December 5, 1955.

The news traveled like wildfire into every black home. Telephones jangled; people congregated on street corners and in homes and talked. But nothing was done. A numbing helplessness seemed to paralyze everyone. Very few stayed off the buses the rest of that day or the next. There was fear, discontent, and uncertainty. Everyone seemed to wait for someone to *do* something, but nobody made a move. For that day and a half, black Americans rode the buses as before, as if nothing had happened. They were sullen and uncommunicative, but they rode the buses. There was a silent, tension-filled waiting. For blacks were not talking loudly in public places—they were quiet, sullen, waiting. Just waiting! Thursday evening came and went.

Thursday night was far spent, when, at about 11:30 P.M., I sat alone in my peaceful single-family dwelling on a quiet street. I was thinking about the situation. Lost in thought, I was startled by the telephone's ring. Black attorney Fred Gray, who had been out of town all day, had just gotten back and was returning the phone message I had left for him about Mrs. Parks's arrest. Attorney Gray, though a very young man, had been one of my most active colleagues in our previous meetings with bus company officials and Commissioner Birmingham. A Montgomery native who had attended Alabama State and been one of my students, Fred Gray had gone on to law school in Ohio before returning to his home town to open a practice with the only other black lawyer in Montgomery, Charles Langford.

Fred Gray and his wife Bernice were good friends of mine, and we talked often. In addition to being a lawyer, Gray was a trained, ordained minister of the gospel, actively serving as assistant pastor of Holt Street Church of Christ.

Tonight his voice on the phone was very short and to the point. Fred was shocked by the news of Mrs. Parks's arrest. I informed him that I already was thinking that the WPC should distribute thousands of notices calling for all bus riders to stay off the buses on Monday, the day of Mrs. Parks's trial. "Are you ready?" he asked. Without hesitation, I assured him that we were. With that he hung up, and I went to work.

I made some notes on the back of an envelope: "The Women's Political Council will not wait for Mrs. Parks's consent to call for a boycott of city buses. On Friday, December 2, 1955, the women of Montgomery will call for a boycott to take place on Monday, December 5."

Some of the WPC officers previously had discussed plans for distributing thousands of notices announcing a bus boycott. Now the time had come for me to write just such a notice. I sat down and quickly drafted a message and then called a good friend and colleague, John Cannon, chairman of the business department at the college, who had access to the college's mimeograph equipment. When I told him that the WPC was staging a boycott and needed to run off the notices, he told me that he too had suffered embarrassment on the city buses. Like myself, he had been hurt and angry. He said that he would happily assist me. Along with two of my most trusted senior students, we quickly agreed to meet almost immediately, in the middle of the night, at the college's duplicating room. We were able to get three messages to a page, greatly reducing the number of pages that had to be mimeographed in order to produce the tens of thousands of leaflets we knew would be needed. By 4 A.M. Friday, the sheets had been duplicated, cut in thirds, and bundled. Each leaflet read:

> Another Negro woman has been arrested and thrown in jail because she refused to get up out of her seat on the bus for a white person to sit down. It is the second time since the Claudette Colvin case that a Negro woman has been arrested for the same thing. This has to be stopped. Negroes have rights, too, for if Negroes did not ride the buses, they could not operate. Three-fourths of the riders are Negroes, yet we are arrested, or have to stand over empty seats. If we do not do something to stop these arrests, they will continue. The next time it may be you, or your daughter, or mother. This woman's case will come up on Monday. We are, therefore, asking every Negro to stay off the buses Monday in protest of the arrest and trial. Don't ride the buses to work, to town, to school, or anywhere on Monday. You can afford to stay out of school for one day if you have no other way to go except by bus. You can also afford to stay out of town for one day. If you work, take a cab, or walk. But please, children and grownups, don't ride the bus at all on Monday. Please stay off of all buses Monday. . . .

When the question was posed as to whether the people would end the one-day bus boycott, thousands of voices shouted the same word, "No! No!" One lone voice cried out in clear tones, "This is just the beginning!" Thunderous applause was the response.

9. ALLEN GINSBERG

Howl

(1956)

Originally printed as a chapbook for City Lights Press, **ALLEN GINS-BERG**'s *Howl* has become one of the most widely read poems of all time. Ginsberg (1926–1997) was born in Newark, New Jersey, and attended Columbia University. In 1949, Ginsberg underwent psychiatric counseling at Rockland State Hospital, where he met Carl Solomon, to whom *Howl* is dedicated. The publication of *Howl* in 1956 is often used to signify the arrival of the Beat Generation, a group of alienated young people who expressed contempt for sterile mainstream society and bourgeois values. The poem's publication also led to a widely publicized "obscenity trial," and the eventual verdict was that the book was not obscene. In the 1960s, Ginsberg identified with the antiwar movement. Although controversial, Ginsberg nevertheless received great acclaim from the literary world before his death, winning a Guggenheim Fellowship, a National Endowment for the Arts grant, and a National Arts Club Gold Medal.

SOURCE: Allen Ginsberg. *Howl and Other Poems.* San Francisco: City Lights Books, 1956.

SELECTED READINGS: Thomas F. Merrill, *Allen Ginsberg* (1988). Lewis Hyde, ed., *On the Poetry of Allen Ginsberg* (1984). John Tytell, *Naked Angels: The Lives and Literature of the Beat Generation* (1976).

For Carl Solomon

I

I saw the best minds of my generation destroyed by
        madness, starving hysterical naked,
dragging themselves through the negro streets at dawn
        looking for an angry fix,
angelheaded hipsters burning for the ancient heavenly
        connection to the starry dynamo in the machinery of night,
who poverty and tatters and hollow-eyed and high sat
        up smoking in the supernatural darkness of
        cold-water flats floating across the tops of cities
        contemplating jazz,
who bared their brains to Heaven under the El and
        saw Mohammedan angels staggering on tenement roofs
        illuminated,
who passed through universities with radiant cool eyes
        hallucinating Arkansas and Blake-light tragedy
        among the scholars of war,
who were expelled from the academies for crazy &
        publishing obscene odes on the windows of the
skull, who cowered in unshaven rooms in underwear, burn-
        ing their money in wastebaskets and listening
        to the Terror through the wall,
who got busted in their pubic beards returning through
        Laredo with a belt of marijuana for New York,
who ate fire in paint hotels or drank turpentine in
        Paradise Alley, death, or purgatoried their
        torsos night after night
with dreams, with drugs, with waking nightmares, al-
        cohol and cock and endless balls, . . .

II

What sphinx of cement and aluminum bashed open
        their skulls and ate up their brains and imagi-
        nation?

Moloch! Solitude! Filth! Ugliness! Ashcans and unob-
tainable dollars! Children screaming under the
stairways! Boys sobbing in armies! Old men
weeping in the parks!

Moloch! Moloch! Nightmare of Moloch! Moloch the
loveless! Mental Moloch! Moloch the heavy
judger of men!

Moloch the incomprehensible prison! Moloch the
crossbone soulless jailhouse and Congress of
sorrows! Moloch whose buildings are judgment!
Moloch the vast stone of war! Moloch the stun-
ned governments!

Moloch whose mind is pure machinery! Moloch whose
blood is running money! Moloch whose fingers
are ten armies! Moloch whose breast is a canni-
bal dynamo! Moloch whose ear is a smoking tomb!

Moloch whose eyes are a thousand blind windows!
Moloch whose skyscrapers stand in the long
streets like endless Jehovahs! Moloch whose fac-
tories dream and croak in the fog! Moloch whose
smokestacks and antennae crown the cities!

Moloch whose love is endless oil and stone! Moloch
whose soul is electricity and banks! Moloch
whose poverty is the specter of genius! Moloch
whose fate is a cloud of sexless hydrogen!
Moloch whose name is the Mind!

Moloch in whom I sit lonely! Moloch in whom I dream
Angels! Crazy in Moloch! Cocksucker in
Moloch! Lacklove and manless in Moloch!

Moloch who entered my soul early! Moloch in whom
I am a consciousness without a body! Moloch
who frightened me out of my natural ecstasy!
Moloch whom I abandon! Wake up in Moloch!
Light streaming out of the sky!

Moloch! Moloch! Robot apartments! invisible suburbs!
skeleton treasuries! blind capitals! demonic

industries! spectral nations! invincible mad
    houses! granite cocks! monstrous bombs!
They broke their backs lifting Moloch to Heaven! Pave-
    ments, trees, radios, tons! lifting the city to
    Heaven which exists and is everywhere about us!
Visions! omens! hallucinations! miracles! ecstasies!
    gone down the American river!
Dreams! adorations! illuminations! religions! the whole
    boatload of sensitive bullshit!
Breakthroughs! over the river! flips and crucifixions!
    gone down the flood! Highs! Epiphanies! De-
    spairs! Ten years' animal screams and suicides!
    Minds! New loves! Mad generation! down on
    the rocks of Time!
Real holy laughter in the river! They saw it all! the
    wild eyes! the holy yells! They bade farewell!
    They jumped off the roof! to solitude! waving!
    carrying flowers! Down to the river! into the street!

III

Carl Solomon! I'm with you in Rockland
    where you're madder than I am
I'm with you in Rockland
    where you must feel very strange
I'm with you in Rockland
    where you imitate the shade of my mother
I'm with you in Rockland
    where you've murdered your twelve secretaries
I'm with you in Rockland
    where you laugh at this invisible humor
I'm with you in Rockland
    where we are great writers on the same dreadful
    typewriter
I'm with you in Rockland
    where your condition has become serious and
    is reported on the radio

I'm with you in Rockland
> where the faculties of the skull no longer admit
> the worms of the senses

I'm with you in Rockland
> where you drink the tea of the breasts of the
> spinsters of Utica

I'm with you in Rockland
> where you pun on the bodies of your nurses the
> harpies of the Bronx

I'm with you in Rockland
> where you scream in a straightjacket that you're
> losing the game of the actual pingpong of the
> abyss

I'm with you in Rockland
> where you bang on the catatonic piano the soul
> is innocent and immortal it should never die
> ungodly in an armed madhouse

I'm with you in Rockland
> where fifty more shocks will never return your
> soul to its body again from its pilgrimage to a
> cross in the void

I'm with you in Rockland
> where you accuse your doctors of insanity and
> plot the Hebrew socialist revolution against the
> fascist national Golgotha

I'm with you in Rockland
> where you will split the heavens of Long Island
> and resurrect your living human Jesus from the
> superhuman tomb

I'm with you in Rockland
> where there are twenty-five-thousand mad com-
> rades all together singing the final stanzas of
> the Internationale

I'm with you in Rockland
> where we hug and kiss the United States under

our bedsheets the United States that coughs all
night and won't let us sleep
I'm with you in Rockland
where we wake up electrified out of the coma
by our own souls' airplanes roaring over the
roof they've come to drop angelic bombs the
hospital illuminates itself imaginary walls collapse O skinny legions run outside O starry-
spangled shock of mercy the eternal war is
here O victory forget your underwear we're
free
I'm with you in Rockland
in my dreams you walk dripping from a sea
journey on the highway across America in tears
to the door of my cottage in the Western night

San Francisco 1955–56

10. STUDENTS FOR A DEMOCRATIC SOCIETY (SDS)

The Port Huron Statement
(1962)

The Port Huron Statement is the major political document of the New Left. Although it was written collectively by a group of nearly sixty radicals at a United Auto Workers retreat in Port Huron, Michigan, in June 1962, its primary author was Tom Hayden (1939–). Inspired by the critical sociology of C. Wright Mills and the African-American sit-in struggle, as well as less obviously political sources such as French existentialism and Beat poetry, the Port Huron Statement greatly shaped the early intellectual development of **STUDENTS FOR A DEMO-CRATIC SOCIETY (SDS)**, the premier New Left organization of the 1960s. Among other things, the document criticized American society for its conformity, militarism, and racism, and it endorsed the civil rights, labor, and peace movements. It also introduced the concept of "participatory democracy"—the notion that individuals should have a say in the decisions that affect their lives. Its opening salvo, "We are people of this generation, bred in at least modest comfort, housed now in universities, looking uncomfortably to the world we inherit," is probably the most oft-quoted line in the literature of the New Left.

SOURCE: James Miller. *"Democracy Is in the Streets": From Port Huron to the Siege of Chicago.* New York: Simon and Schuster, 1987.

SELECTED READINGS: Tom Hayden, *Reunion: A Memoir* (1988). James Miller, *"Democracy Is in the Streets": From Port Huron to the Siege of Chicago* (1987). Kirkpatrick Sale, *SDS* (1971).

Introduction: Agenda for a Generation

We are people of this generation, bred in at least modest comfort, housed now in universities, looking uncomfortably to the world we inherit.

When we were kids the United States was the wealthiest and strongest country in the world; the only one with the atom bomb, the least scarred by modern war, an initiator of the United Nations that we thought would distribute Western influence throughout the world. Freedom and equality for each individual, government of, by, and for the people—these American values we found good, principles by which we could live as men. Many of us began maturing in complacency.

As we grew, however, our comfort was penetrated by events too troubling to dismiss. First, the permeating and victimizing fact of human degradation, symbolized by the Southern struggle against racial bigotry, compelled most of us from silence to activism. Second, the enclosing fact of the Cold War, symbolized by the presence of the Bomb, brought awareness that we ourselves, and our friends, and millions of abstract "others" we knew more directly because of our common peril, might die at any time. We might deliberately ignore, or avoid, or fail to feel all other human problems, but not these two, for these were too immediate and crushing in their impact, too challenging in the demand that we as individuals take the responsibility for encounter and resolution.

While these and other problems either directly oppressed us or rankled our consciences and became our own subjective concerns, we began to see complicated and disturbing paradoxes in our surrounding America. The declaration "all men are created equal . . ." rang hollow before the facts of Negro life in the South and the big cities of the North. The proclaimed peaceful intentions of the United

States contradicted its economic and military investments in the Cold War status quo.

We witnessed, and continue to witness, other paradoxes. With nuclear energy whole cities can easily be powered, yet the dominant nation-states seem more likely to unleash destruction greater than that incurred in all wars of human history. Although our own technology is destroying old and creating new forms of social organization, men still tolerate meaningless work and idleness. While two-thirds of mankind suffers undernourishment, our own upper classes revel amidst superfluous abundance. Although world population is expected to double in forty years, the nations still tolerate anarchy as a major principle of international conduct and uncontrolled exploitation governs the sapping of the earth's physical resources. Although mankind desperately needs revolutionary leadership, America rests in national stalemate, its goals ambiguous and tradition-bound instead of informed and clear, its democratic system apathetic and manipulated rather than "of, by, and for the people."

Not only did tarnish appear on our image of American virtue, not only did disillusion occur when the hypocrisy of American ideals was discovered, but we began to sense that what we had originally seen as the American Golden Age was actually the decline of an era. The world-wide outbreak of revolution against colonialism and imperialism, the entrenchment of totalitarian states, the menace of war, overpopulation, international disorder, supertechnology—these trends were testing the tenacity of our own commitment to democracy and freedom and our abilities to visualize their application to a world in upheaval.

Our work is guided by the sense that we may be the last generation in the experiment with living. But we are a minority—the vast majority of our people regard the temporary equilibriums of our society and world as eternally functional parts. In this is perhaps the outstanding paradox: we ourselves are imbued with urgency, yet the message of our society is that there is no viable alternative to the present. Beneath the reassuring tones of the politicians, beneath the common opinion that America will "muddle through," beneath the stagnation of those who have closed their minds to the future, is the pervading feeling that there simply are no alternatives, that our times have witnessed the exhaustion not only of Utopias, but of any new departures as well. Feeling the press of complexity upon the emptiness of life, people are fearful of the thought that at any moment things might be thrust out of control. They fear change itself, since change might smash whatever invisible framework seems to hold back chaos for them now. For most Americans, all crusades are suspect, threatening. The fact that each individual sees apathy in his fellows perpetuates the common reluctance to organize for change. The dominant institutions are complex enough to blunt the minds of their potential critics, and entrenched enough to swiftly dissipate or entirely repel the energies of protest and reform, thus limiting human expectancies. Then, too, we are a materially improved society, and by our own improvements we seem to have weakened the case for further change.

Some would have us believe that Americans feel contentment amidst prosperity—but might it not better be called a glaze above deeply felt anxieties about their role in the new world? And if these anxieties produce a developed indifference to human affairs, do they not as well produce a yearning to believe there *is* an alternative to the present, that something *can* be done to change circumstances in the school, the workplaces, the bureaucracies, the government? It is to this latter yearning, at once the spark and engine of change, that we direct our present appeal. The search for truly democratic alternatives to the present, and a commitment to social experimentation with them, is a worthy and fulfilling human enterprise, one which moves us and, we hope, others today. On such a basis do we offer this document of our convictions and analysis: as an effort in understanding and changing the conditions of humanity in the late twentieth century, an effort rooted in the ancient, still unfulfilled conception of man attaining determining influence over his circumstances of life. . . .

The Students

In the last few years, thousands of American students demonstrated that they at least felt the urgency of the times. They moved actively and directly against racial injustices, the threat of war, violations of individual rights of conscience, and, less frequently, against economic manipulation. They succeeded in restoring a small measure of controversy to the campuses after the stillness of the McCarthy period. They succeeded, too, in gaining some concessions from the people and institutions they opposed, especially in the fight against racial bigotry.

The significance of these scattered movements lies not in their success or failure in gaining objectives—at least, not yet. Nor does the significance lie in the intellectual "competence" or "maturity" of the students involved—as some pedantic elders allege. The significance is in the fact that students are breaking the crust of apathy and overcoming the inner alienation that remain the defining characteristics of American college life.

If student movements for change are still rarities on the campus scene, what is commonplace there? The real campus, the familiar campus, is a place of private people, engaged in their notorious "inner emigration." It is a place of commitment to business-as-usual, getting ahead, playing it cool. It is a place of mass affirmation of the Twist, but mass reluctance toward the controversial public stance. Rules are accepted as "inevitable," bureaucracy as "just circumstances," irrelevance as "scholarship," selflessness as "martyrdom," politics as "just another way to make people, and an unprofitable one, too."

Almost no students value activity as citizens. Passive in public, they are hardly more idealistic in arranging their private lives: Gallup concludes they will settle for "low success, and won't risk high failure." There is not much willingness to take risks (not even in business), no setting of dangerous goals, no real conception of personal identity except one manufactured in the image of others, no real urge for personal fulfillment except to be almost as successful as the very successful people. Attention is being paid to social status (the quality of shirt collars, meeting people, getting wives or husbands, making solid contacts for later on); much, too, is paid to academic status (grades, honors, the med school rat race). But neglected generally is real intellectual status, the personal cultivation of the mind.

"Students don't even give a damn about the apathy," one has said. Apathy toward apathy begets a privately constructed universe, a place of systematic study schedules, two nights each week for beer, a girl or two, and early marriage; a framework infused with personality, warmth, and under control, no matter how unsatisfying otherwise.

Under these conditions university life loses all relevance to some. Four hundred thousand of our classmates leave college every year.

But apathy is not simply an attitude; it is a product of social institutions, and of the structure and organization of higher education itself. The extracurricular life is ordered according to *in loco parentis* theory, which ratifies the Administration as the moral guardian of the young.

The accompanying "let's pretend" theory of student extracurricular affairs validates student government as a training center for those who want to spend their lives in political pretense, and discourages initiative from the more articulate, honest, and sensitive students. The bounds and style of controversy are delimited before controversy begins. The university "prepares" the student for "citizenship" through perpetual rehearsals and, usually, through emasculation of what creative spirit there is in the individual.

The academic life contains reinforcing counterparts to the way in which extracurricular life is organized. The academic world is founded on a teacher-student relation analogous to the parent-child relation which characterizes *in loco parentis*. Further, academia includes a radical separation of the student from the material of study. That which is studied, the social reality, is "objectified" to sterility, dividing the student from life—just as he is restrained in active involvement by the deans controlling student government. The specialization of function and knowledge, admittedly necessary to our complex technological and social structure, has produced an exaggerated compartmentalization of study and understanding. This has contributed to an overly parochial view, by faculty, of the role of its research and scholarship; to a discontinuous and truncated understanding, by students, of the surrounding social order; and to a loss of personal attachment, by nearly all, to the worth of study as a humanistic enterprise.

There is, finally, the cumbersome academic bureaucracy extending throughout the academic as well as the extracurricular structures, contributing to the sense of outer complexity and inner powerlessness that transforms the honest searching of many students to a ratification of convention and, worse, to a numbness to present and future catastrophes. The size and financing systems of the university enhance the permanent trusteeship of the administrative bureaucracy, their power leading to a shift within the university toward the value standards of business and the administrative mentality. Huge foundations and other private financial interests shape the under-financed colleges and universities, making them not only more commercial, but less disposed to diagnose society critically, less open to dissent. Many social and physical scientists, neglecting the liberating heritage of higher learning, develop "human relations" or "morale-producing" techniques for the corporate economy, while others exercise their intellectual skills to accelerate the arms race.

Tragically, the university could serve as a significant source of social criticism and an initiator of new modes and molders of attitudes. But the actual intellectual effect of the college experience is hardly distinguishable from that of any other communications channel—say, a television set—passing on the stock truths of the day. Students leave college somewhat more "tolerant" than when they arrived, but basically unchallenged in their values and political orientations. With administrators ordering the institution, and faculty, the curriculum, the student learns by his isolation to accept elite rule within the university, which prepares him to accept later forms of minority control. The real function of the educational system—as opposed to its more rhetorical function of "searching for truth"—is to impart the key information and styles that will help the student get by, modestly but comfortably, in the big society beyond.

The Society Beyond

Look beyond the campus, to America itself. That student life is more intellectual, and perhaps more comfortable, does not obscure the fact that the fundamental qualities of life on the campus reflect the habits of society at large. The fraternity president is seen at the junior manager levels; the sorority queen has gone to Grosse Pointe; the serious poet burns for a place, any place, to work; the once-serious and never-serious poets work at the advertising agencies. The desperation of people threatened by forces about which they know little and of which they can say less; the cheerful emptiness of people "giving up" all hope of changing things; the faceless ones polled by Gallup who listed "international affairs" fourteenth on their list of "problems" but who also expected thermo-nuclear war in the next few years; in these and other forms, Americans are in withdrawal from public life, from any collective effort at directing their own affairs.

Some regard these national doldrums as a sign of healthy approval of the established order—but is it approval by consent or manipulated acquiescence? Others declare that the people are withdrawn because compelling issues are fast disappearing—perhaps there are fewer breadlines in America, but is Jim Crow gone, is there enough work and work more fulfilling, is world war a diminishing threat, and what of the revolutionary new peoples? Still others think the national quietude is a necessary consequence of the need for elites to resolve complex and specialized problems of modern industrial society—but, then, why should *business* elites help decide foreign policy, and who controls the elites anyway, and are they solving mankind's problems? Others, finally, shrug knowingly and announce that full democracy never worked anywhere in the past—but why lump qualitatively different civilizations together, and how can a social order work well if its best thinkers are skeptics, and is man really doomed forever to the domination of today?

There are no convincing apologies for the contemporary malaise. While the world tumbles toward the final war, while men in other nations are trying desperately to alter events, while the very future qua future is uncertain—America is without community impulse, without the inner momentum necessary for an age when societies cannot successfully perpetuate themselves by their military weapons, when democracy must be viable because of its quality of life, not its quantity of rockets.

The apathy here is, first, *subjective*—the felt powerlessness of ordinary people, the resignation before the enormity of events. But subjective apathy is encouraged by the *objective* American situation—the actual structural separation of people from power, from relevant knowledge, from pinnacles of decision-making. Just as the university influences the student way of life, so do major social institutions create the circumstances in which the isolated citizen will try hopelessly to understand his world and himself.

The very isolation of the individual—from power and community and ability to aspire—means the rise of a democracy without publics. With the great mass of people structurally remote and psychologically hesitant with respect to democratic institutions, those institutions themselves attenuate and become, in the fashion of the vicious circle, progressively less accessible to those few who aspire to serious participation in social affairs. The vital democratic connection between community and leadership, between the mass and the several elites, has been so wrenched and perverted that disastrous policies go unchallenged time and again. . . .

University and Social Change

There is perhaps little reason to be optimistic about the above analysis. True, the Dixiecrat-GOP coalition is the weakest point in the dominating complex of corporate, military, and political power. But the civil rights, peace, and student movements are too poor and socially slighted, and the labor movement too quiescent, to be counted with enthusiasm. From where else can power and vision be summoned? We believe that the universities are an overlooked seat of influence.

First, the university is located in a permanent position of social influence. Its educational function makes it indispensable and automatically makes it a crucial institution in the formation of social attitudes. Second, in an unbelievably complicated world, it is the central institution for organizing, evaluating, and transmitting knowledge. Third, the extent to which academic resources presently are used to buttress immoral social practice is revealed, first, by the extent to which defense contracts make the universities engineers of the arms race. Too, the use of modern social science as a manipulative tool reveals itself in the "human relations" consultants to the modern corporations, who introduce trivial sops to give laborers feelings of "participation" or "belonging," while actually deluding them in order to further exploit their labor. And, of course, the use of motivational research is already infamous as a manipulative aspect of American politics. But these social uses of the universities' resources also demonstrate the unchangeable reliance by men of power on the men and storehouses of knowledge: this makes the university functionally tied to society in new ways, revealing new potentialities, new levers for change. Fourth, the university is the only mainstream institution that is open to participation by individuals of nearly any viewpoint.

These, at least, are facts, no matter how dull the teaching, how paternalistic the rules, how irrelevant the research that goes on. Social relevance, the accessibility to knowledge, and internal openness—these together make the university a potential base and agency in a movement of social change.

1. Any new left in America must be, in large measure, a left with real intellectual skills, committed to deliberativeness, honesty, reflection as working tools. The university permits the political life to be an adjunct to the academic one, and action to be informed by reason.

2. A new left must be distributed in significant social roles throughout the country. The universities are distributed in such a manner.

3. A new left must consist of younger people who matured in the postwar world, and partially be directed to the recruitment of younger people. The university is an obvious beginning point.

4. A new left must include liberals and socialists, the former for their relevance, the latter for their sense of thoroughgoing reforms in the system. The university is a more sensible place than a political party for these two traditions to begin to discuss their differences and look for political synthesis.

5. A new left must start controversy across the land, if national policies and national apathy are to be reversed. The ideal university is a community of controversy, within itself and in its effects on communities beyond.

6. A new left must transform modern complexity into issues that can be understood and felt close up by every human being. It must give form to the feelings of helplessness and indifference, so that people may see the political, social, and economic sources of their private troubles and organize to change society. In a time of supposed

prosperity, moral complacency, and political manipulation, a new left cannot rely on only aching stomachs to be the engine force of social reform. The case for change, for alternatives that will involve uncomfortable personal efforts, must be argued as never before. The university is a relevant place for all of these activities.

But we need not indulge in illusions: the university system cannot complete a movement of ordinary people making demands for a better life. From its schools and colleges across the nation, a militant left might awaken its allies, and by beginning the process towards peace, civil rights, and labor struggles, reinsert theory and idealism where too often reign confusion and political barter. The power of students and faculty united is not only potential; it has shown its actuality in the South, and in the reform movements of the North.

The bridge to political power, though, will be built through genuine cooperation, locally, nationally, and internationally, between a new left of young people and an awakening community of allies. In each community we must look within the university and act with confidence that we can be powerful, but we must look outwards to the less exotic but more lasting struggles for justice.

To turn these possibilities into realities will involve national efforts at university reform by an alliance of students and faculty. They must wrest control of the educational process from the administrative bureaucracy. They must make fraternal and functional contact with allies in labor, civil rights, and other liberal forces outside the campus. They must import major public issues into the curriculum— research and teaching on problems of war and peace is an outstanding example. They must make debate and controversy, not dull pedantic cant, the common style for educational life. They must consciously build a base for their assault upon the loci of power.

As students for a democratic society, we are committed to stimulating this kind of social movement, this kind of vision and program in campus and community across the country. If we appear to seek the unattainable, as it has been said, then let it be known that we do so to avoid the unimaginable.

11. RACHEL CARSON

Silent Spring
(1962)

The beginning of the environmental movement of the 1960s is often dated to the publication of **RACHEL CARSON**'s *Silent Spring* in 1962. Carson (1907–1964) was born in Springfield, Pennsylvania, and she earned an M.A. in zoology from Johns Hopkins University in 1932. In 1935, she began working for the U.S. Bureau of Fisheries, and she wrote several books, including *The Sea Around Us* (1951) and *The Edge of the Sea* (1955). Carson began researching the lethal dangers of pesticides (especially DDT) after she learned that municipal aerial spraying near Boston had caused the death of neighborhood songbirds. Although *Silent Spring* provoked fierce criticism from some industry spokesmen and government officials, the science that informed the book was later shown to be sound. *Silent Spring* became a worldwide bestseller, and it inspired further research on environmental pollution. Carson died of cancer in 1964.

SOURCE: Rachel Carson. *Silent Spring.* Boston: Houghton Mifflin Company, 1962.

SELECTED READINGS: Thomas R. Dunlap, ed., *DDT,* Silent Spring, *and the Rise of Environmentalism* (2008); foreword by William Cronon. Lisa H. Sideris and Kathleen Dean Moore, eds., *Rachel Carson: Legacy and*

Challenge (2008). Mark H. Lytle, *The Gentle Subversive: Rachel Carson,* Silent Spring, *and the Rise of the Environmental Movement* (2007).

The history of life on earth has been a history of interaction between living things and their surroundings. To a large extent, the physical form and the habits of the earth's vegetation and its animal life have been molded by the environment. Considering the whole span of earthly time, the opposite effect, in which life actually modifies its surroundings, has been relatively slight. Only within the moment of time represented by the present century has one species—man—acquired significant power to alter the nature of his world.

During the past quarter century this power has not only increased to one of disturbing magnitude but it has changed in character. The most alarming of all man's assaults upon the environment is the contamination of air, earth, rivers, and sea with dangerous and even lethal materials. This pollution is for the most part irrecoverable; the chain of evil it initiates not only in the world that must support life but in living tissues is for the most part irreversible. In this now universal contamination of the environment, chemicals are the sinister and little-recognized partners of radiation in changing the very nature of the world—the very nature of its life. Strontium 90, released through nuclear explosions into the air, comes to earth in rain or drifts down as fallout, lodges in soil, enters into the grass or corn or wheat grown there, and in time takes up its abode in the bones of a human being, there to remain until his death. Similarly, chemicals sprayed on croplands or forests or gardens lie long in soil, entering into living organisms, passing from one to another in a chain of poisoning and death. Or they pass mysteriously by underground streams until they emerge and, through the alchemy of air and sunlight, combine into new forms that kill vegetation, sicken cattle, and work unknown harm on those who drink from once pure wells. As Albert Schweitzer has said, "Man can hardly even recognize the devils of his own creation."

It took hundreds of millions of years to produce the life that now inhabits the earth—eons of time in which that developing and evolving and diversifying life reached a state of adjustment and balance with its surroundings. The environment, rigorously shaping and directing the life it supported, contained elements that were hostile as well as supporting. Certain rocks gave out dangerous radiation; even within the light of the sun, from which all life draws its energy, there were short-wave radiations with power to injure. Given time—time not in years but in millennia—life adjusts, and a balance has been reached. For time is the essential ingredient; but in the modern world there is no time.

The rapidity of change and the speed with which new situations are created follow the impetuous and heedless pace of man rather than the deliberate pace of nature. Radiation is no longer merely the background radiation of rocks, the bombardment of cosmic rays, the ultraviolet of the sun that have existed before there was any life on earth; radiation is now the unnatural creation of man's tampering with the atom. The chemicals to which life is asked to make its adjustment are no longer merely the calcium and silica and copper and all the rest of the minerals washed out of the rocks and carried in rivers to the sea; they are the synthetic creations of man's inventive mind, brewed in his laboratories, and having no counterparts in nature.

To adjust to these chemicals would require time on the scale that is nature's; it would require not merely the years of a man's life but the life of generations. And even this, were it by some miracle possible, would be futile, for the new chemicals come from our laboratories in an endless stream; almost five hundred annually find their way into actual use in the United States alone. The figure is staggering and its implications are not easily grasped—500 new chemicals to which the bodies of men and animals are required somehow to adapt each year, chemicals totally outside the limits of biologic experience.

Among them are many that are used in man's war against nature. Since the mid-1940s over 200 basic chemicals have been created for use in killing insects, weeds, rodents, and other organisms described in the modern vernacular as "pests"; and they are sold under several thousand different brand names.

These sprays, dusts, and aerosols are now applied almost universally to farms, gardens, forests, and homes—nonselective chemicals that have the power to kill every insect, the "good" and the "bad," to still the song of birds and the leaping of fish in the streams, to coat the leaves with a deadly film, and to linger on in soil—all this though the intended target may be only a few weeds or insects. Can anyone believe it is possible to lay down such a barrage of poisons on the surface of the earth without making it unfit for all life? They should not be called "insecticides," but "biocides."

The whole process of spraying seems caught up in an endless spiral. Since DDT was released for civilian use, a process of escalation has been going on in which ever more toxic materials must be found. This has happened because insects, in a triumphant vindication of Darwin's principle of the survival of the fittest, have evolved super races immune to the particular insecticide used, hence a deadlier one has always to be developed—and then a deadlier one than that. It has happened also because, for reasons to be described later, destructive insects often undergo a "flareback," or resurgence, after spraying, in numbers greater than before. Thus the chemical war is never won, and all life is caught in its violent crossfire.

Along with the possibility of the extinction of mankind by nuclear war, the central problem of our age has therefore become the contamination of man's total environment with such substances of incredible potential for harm—substances that accumulate in the tissues of plants and animals and even penetrate the germ cells to shatter or alter the very material of heredity upon which the shape of the future depends.

Some would-be architects of our future look toward a time when it will be possible to alter the human germ plasm by design. But we may easily be doing so now by inadvertence, for many chemicals, like radiation, bring about gene mutations. It is ironic to think that man might determine his own future by something so seemingly trivial as the choice of an insect spray.

All this has been risked—for what? Future historians may well be amazed by our distorted sense of proportion. How could intelligent beings seek to control a few unwanted species by a method that contaminated the entire environment and brought the threat of disease and death even to their own kind? Yet this is precisely what we have done. We have done it, moreover, for reasons that collapse the moment we examine them. We are told that the enormous and expanding use of pesticides is necessary to maintain farm production. Yet is our real problem not one of *overproduction?* Our farms, despite measures to remove acreages from production and to pay farmers *not* to produce, have yielded such a staggering excess of crops that the American taxpayer in 1962 is paying out more than one billion dollars a year as the total carrying cost of the *surplus-food* storage program. And is the situation helped when one branch of the Agriculture Department tries to reduce production while another states, as it did in 1958, "It is believed generally that reduction of crop acreages under provisions of the Soil Bank will stimulate interest in use of chemicals to obtain maximum production on the land retained in crops"?

All this is not to say there is no insect problem and no need of control. I am saying, rather, that control must be geared to realities, not to mythical situations, and that the methods employed must be such that they do not destroy us along with the insects.

12. BETTY FRIEDAN

The Feminine Mystique
(1963)

BETTY FRIEDAN's 1963 book *The Feminine Mystique* is often credited with reviving organized modern feminism. Friedan (1921–2006) was educated at Smith College and the University of California at Berkeley. In 1966 she founded the National Organization for Women (NOW), and she served as president of that organization until 1970. She also helped found the National Women's Political Caucus in 1971. In *The Feminine Mystique*, Friedan argued against the widely held belief that women could find fulfillment only through childbearing, mothering, and homemaking. Beneath the 1950s image of the "happy suburban housewife," Friedan found a great deal of discontentment. *The Feminine Mystique* was enormously well-received by millions of quietly desperate housewives, and as a result, Friedan has been called the "Susan B. Anthony of a newly revitalized women's movement."

SOURCE: Betty Friedan. *The Feminine Mystique*. New York: W. W. Norton & Co., 1963.

SELECTED READINGS: Betty Friedan, *Life So Far* (2000). Judith Adler Hennessee, *Betty Friedan: Her Life* (1999). Daniel Horowitz, *Betty Friedan and the Making of the Feminine Mystique: The American Left, the Cold War, and Modern Feminism* (1989).

Chapter 1
"The Problem That Has No Name"

Gradually, I came to realize that something is wrong with the way American women are trying to live their lives today. I sensed it first, as a question mark in my own life, as a wife and mother of three small children, half-guiltily and half-heartedly using my abilities and education that took me away from home. It was this personal question mark that led me in 1957 to my college classmates, fifteen years after our graduation from Smith. The problems and satisfaction of their lives and mine did not fit the image of the modern American woman written about in magazines [and] studied in classrooms and clinics. There was a discrepancy between the reality of our lives and the image to which we were trying to conform, the image I call the feminine mystique. I wondered if other women faced this schizophrenic split. And so I began to hunt down the origins of the feminine mystique, and its effect on women who lived by it, or grew up under it.

The problem lay buried, unspoken, for many years in the minds of American women. It was a sense of dissatisfaction, a yearning. Each suburban housewife struggled with it alone as she made beds, shopped for groceries, matched slipcover material, ate peanut butter sandwiches with her children, chauffeured Cub Scouts and Brownies, lay beside her husband at night—she was afraid to ask the silent question—"Is this all?"

For fifteen years [following World War II] in books and articles by experts, women heard that they could desire no greater destiny than to glory in their own femininity. Experts told them how to catch a man and keep him, how to breastfeed children and handle their toilet training, how to buy a dishwasher, bake bread, cook gourmet snails; how to dress, look, and act more feminine and make marriage more exciting. They were taught to pity the neurotic, unfeminine, unhappy women who wanted to be poets or physicists or presidents. They learned that feminine women did not want careers, higher education, political rights—the independence and opportunities that the old-fashioned feminists fought for.

The suburban housewife—she was the dream of young American women and the envy of women all over the world. She was healthy, beautiful, educated, concerned only about her husband, her children, her home. She had found true feminine fulfillment, free to choose automobiles, clothes, appliances, supermarkets; she had everything that women everywhere dreamed of.

Millions lived the image of the suburban housewife, kissing their husbands goodbye, depositing children at school, smiling as they ran the new waxer over the spotless kitchen floor. They baked bread, sewed their and their children's clothes, kept new washing machines and dryers running all day. They changed the sheets on the bed twice a week, took the rug-hooking class, and pitied their poor frustrated mothers who had dreamed of having a career. Their only dream was to be perfect wives and mothers; their highest ambition to have five children and a beautiful house; their only fight to get and keep their husbands.

If a woman had a problem in the 1950s and 1960s, she knew that something must be wrong with her marriage, or with herself. Other women were satisfied with their lives. What kind of woman was she if she did not feel this mysterious fulfillment waxing the kitchen floor? She was so ashamed to admit her dissatisfaction that she never knew how many other women shared it. Women found it harder to talk about this problem than about sex.

But on an April morning in 1959, I heard a mother of four, having coffee with four other mothers in a suburban development, say in a tone of quiet desperation, "the problem." And the others knew without words that she was not talking about a problem with her husband or her children, or her home. Suddenly they realized that they all shared the same problem, the problem that has no name. They began to talk about it.

Just what was this problem that has no name? Sometimes a woman would say "I feel empty." Or she would say, "I feel as if I don't exist." Sometimes she blotted out the feeling with a tranquilizer. Sometimes she thought the problem was with her husband or her children or that what she needed was to redecorate her house, move to a better neighborhood, have an affair, or another baby.

In 1960, the problem that has no name burst like a boil through the image of the happy housewife from the *New York Times* and *Newsweek* to *Good Housekeeping*. Some said the problem [was] education which naturally made [women] unhappy in their role as housewives. "The road from Freud to Frigidaire, from Sophocles to Spock has turned out to be a bumpy one," reported the *New York Times* (June 28, 1960).

Home economists suggested more realistic preparation for housewives, such as high school workshops on home appliances. College educators suggested more discussion groups on home management and the family to prepare women for the adjustment to domestic life.

A number of educators suggested that women no longer be admitted to colleges and universities, [that] the education girls could not use as housewives was needed by boys to do the work of the atomic age.

The problem was dismissed by telling the housewife she doesn't realize how lucky she is—her own boss, no time clock, no junior executive gunning for her job. What if she isn't happy—does she think men are happy? Does she still want to be a man?

The problem was dismissed by shrugging that there are no solutions: this is what being a woman means, and what is wrong with American women that they can't accept their role gracefully?

It is no longer possible to ignore that voice, to dismiss the desperation of so many women. This is not what being a woman means, no matter what the experts say.

It is no longer possible to blame the problem on loss of femininity: to say that education and independence and equality with men have made American women unfeminine.

The problem that has no name is not a matter of loss of femininity, or too much education. It is far more important than anyone recognizes. It may be the key to our future as a nation and a culture. We can no longer ignore that voice within women that says: "I want something more than my husband and my children, and my home."

13. MARTIN LUTHER KING, JR.

Letter from Birmingham Jail
(1963)

MARTIN LUTHER KING, Jr.'s "Letter from Birmingham Jail" is a classic of American protest literature. King (1929–1968) was born in Atlanta, Georgia. After earning his Ph.D. in theology at Boston University, King became minister of Dexter Avenue Baptist Church in Montgomery, Alabama, where he rose to regional prominence as the leader of a boycott of Montgomery's segregated city buses. Later, he organized the Southern Christian Leadership Conference (SCLC) and emerged as a national leader for civil rights. In 1963 he gave his famous "I Have a Dream" speech at the March on Washington, and in 1964 he was awarded the Nobel Peace Prize. In the last years of his life, he began to move leftward politically, focusing greater attention on poverty and speaking out against the Vietnam War. He was assassinated in Memphis, Tennessee, on April 4, 1968. In "Letter from Birmingham Jail," King argued that segregation betrayed America's democratic faith and violated basic Christian principles. The essay had a great impact, boosting support for civil rights across the country.

SOURCE: Martin Luther King, Jr. *Why We Can't Wait.* New York: Harper & Row, 1963.

SELECTED READINGS: Jonathan S. Bass, *Blessed Are the Peacemakers: Martin Luther King, Jr., Eight White Religious Leaders, and the "Letter From*

Birmingham Jail" (2001). Taylor Branch, *Parting the Waters: America in the King Years, 1954–1963* (1988). Diane McWhorter, *Carry Me Home: Birmingham, Alabama: The Climactic Battle of the Civil Rights Revolution* (2001).

April 16, 1963

My Dear Fellow Clergymen:

While confined here in the Birmingham city jail, I came across your recent statement calling my present activities "unwise and untimely." Seldom do I pause to answer criticism of my work and ideas. If I sought to answer all the criticisms that cross my desk, my secretaries would have little time for anything other than such correspondence in the course of the day, and I would have no time for constructive work. But since I feel that you are men of genuine good will and that your criticisms are sincerely set forth, I want to try to answer your statement in what I hope will be patient and reasonable terms.

I think I should indicate why I am here in Birmingham, since you have been influenced by the view which argues against "outsiders coming in." I have the honor of serving as president of the Southern Christian Leadership Conference, an organization operating in every southern state, with headquarters in Atlanta, Georgia. We have some eighty-five affiliated organizations across the South, and one of them is the Alabama Christian Movement for Human Rights. Frequently we share staff [and] educational and financial resources with our affiliates. Several months ago the affiliate here in Birmingham asked us to be on call to engage in a nonviolent direct-action program if such were deemed necessary. We readily consented, and when the hour came we lived up to our promise. So I, along with several members of my staff, am here because I was invited here. I am here because I have organizational ties here.

But more basically, I am in Birmingham because injustice is here. Just as the prophets of the eighth century B.C. left their villages and carried their "thus saith the Lord" far beyond the boundaries of their home towns, and just as the Apostle Paul left his village of Tarsus and carried the gospel of Jesus Christ to the far corners of the Greco-Roman world, so am I compelled to carry the gospel of freedom beyond my own home town. Like Paul, I must constantly respond to the Macedonian call for aid.

Moreover, I am cognizant of the interrelatedness of all communities and states. I cannot sit idly by in Atlanta and not be concerned about what happens in Birmingham. Injustice anywhere is a threat to justice everywhere. We are caught in an inescapable network of mutuality, tied in a single garment of destiny. Whatever affects one directly, affects all indirectly. Never again can we afford to live with the narrow, provincial "outside agitator" idea. Anyone who lives inside the United States can never be considered an outsider anywhere within its bounds.

You deplore the demonstrations taking place in Birmingham. But your statement, I am sorry to say, fails to express a similar concern for the conditions that brought about the demonstrations. I am sure that none of you would want to rest content with the superficial kind of social analysis that deals merely with effects and does not grapple with underlying causes. It is unfortunate that demonstrations are taking place in Birmingham, but it is even more unfortunate that the city's white power structure left the Negro community with no alternative.

In any nonviolent campaign there are four basic steps: collection of the facts to determine whether injustices exist; negotiation; self-purification; and direct action. We have gone through all these steps in Birmingham. There can be no gainsaying the fact that racial injustice engulfs this community. Birmingham is probably the most thoroughly segregated city in the United States. Its ugly record of brutality is widely known. Negroes have experienced grossly unjust treatment in the courts. There have been more unsolved bombings of Negro homes and churches in Birmingham than in any other city in the nation. These are the hard, brutal facts of the case. On the basis of these conditions, Negro leaders sought to negotiate with the city fathers. But the latter consistently refused to engage in good-faith negotiation.

Then, last September, came the opportunity to talk with leaders of Birmingham's economic community. In the course of the negotiations, certain promises were made by the merchants—for example, to remove the stores' humiliating racial signs. On the basis of these promises, the Reverend Fred Shuttlesworth and the leaders of the Alabama Christian Movement for Human Rights agreed to a moratorium on all demonstrations. As the weeks and months went by, we realized that we were the victims of a broken promise. A few signs, briefly removed, returned; the others remained.

As in so many past experiences, our hopes had been blasted, and the shadow of deep disappointment settled upon us. We had no alternative except to prepare for direct action, whereby we would present our very bodies as a means of laying our case before the conscience of the local and the national community. Mindful of the difficulties involved, we decided to undertake a process of self-purification. We began a series of workshops on nonviolence, and we repeatedly asked ourselves: "Are you able to accept blows without retaliating?" "Are you able to endure the ordeal of jail?" We decided to schedule our direct-action program for the Easter season, realizing that except for Christmas, this is the main shopping period of the year. Knowing that a strong economic-withdrawal program would be the by-product of direct action, we felt that this would be the best time to bring pressure to bear on the merchants for the needed change.

Then it occurred to us that Birmingham's mayoralty election was coming up in March, and we speedily decided to postpone action until after election day. When we discovered that the Commissioner of Public Safety, Eugene "Bull" Connor, had piled up enough votes to be in the run-off, we decided again to

postpone action until the day after the runoff so that the demonstrations could not be used to cloud the issues. Like many
others, we waited to see Mr. Connor defeated, and to this end
we endured postponement after postponement. Having aided
in this community need, we felt that our direct-action program
could be delayed no longer.

You may well ask: "Why direct action? Why sit-ins, marches
and so forth? Isn't negotiation a better path?" You are quite
right in calling for negotiation. Indeed, this is the very purpose
of direct action. Nonviolent direct action seeks to create such a
crisis and foster such a tension that a community which has
constantly refused to negotiate is forced to confront the issue. It
seeks so to dramatize the issue that it can no longer be ignored.
My citing the creation of tension as part of the work of the
nonviolent-resister may sound rather shocking. But I must confess that I am not afraid of the word "tension." I have earnestly
opposed violent tension, but there is a type of constructive, nonviolent tension which is necessary for growth. Just as Socrates
felt that it was necessary to create a tension in the mind so that
individuals could rise from the bondage of myths and half-
truths to the unfettered realm of creative analysis and objective
appraisal, so must we see the need for nonviolent gadflies to create the kind of tension in society that will help men rise from
the dark depths of prejudice and racism to the majestic heights
of understanding and brotherhood.

The purpose of our direct-action program is to create a situation so crisis-packed that it will inevitably open the door to
negotiation. I therefore concur with you in your call for negotiation. Too long has our beloved Southland been bogged down
in a tragic effort to live in monologue rather than dialogue.

One of the basic points in your statement is that the action
that I and my associates have taken in Birmingham is untimely. Some have asked: "Why didn't you give the new city
administration time to act?" The only answer that I can give to
this query is that the new Birmingham administration must be
prodded about as much as the outgoing one, before it will act.

We are sadly mistaken if we feel that the election of Albert Boutwell as mayor will bring the millennium to Birmingham. While Mr. Boutwell is a much more gentle person than Mr. Connor, they are both segregationists, dedicated to maintenance of the status quo. I have hope that Mr. Boutwell will be reasonable enough to see the futility of massive resistance to desegregation. But he will not see this without pressure from devotees of civil rights. My friends, I must say to you that we have not made a single gain in civil rights without determined legal and nonviolent pressure. Lamentably, it is an historical fact that privileged groups seldom give up their privileges voluntarily. Individuals may see the moral light and voluntarily give up their unjust posture; but, as Reinhold Niebuhr has reminded us, groups tend to be more immoral than individuals.

We know through painful experience that freedom is never voluntarily given by the oppressor; it must be demanded by the oppressed. Frankly, I have yet to engage in a direct-action campaign that was "well timed" in the view of those who have not suffered unduly from the disease of segregation. For years now I have heard the word "Wait!" It rings in the ear of every Negro with piercing familiarity. This "Wait" has almost always meant "Never." We must come to see, with one of our distinguished jurists, that "justice too long delayed is justice denied."

We have waited for more than 340 years for our constitutional and God-given rights. The nations of Asia and Africa are moving with jetlike speed toward gaining political independence, but we still creep at horse-and-buggy pace toward gaining a cup of coffee at a lunch counter. Perhaps it is easy for those who have never felt the stinging darts of segregation to say, "Wait." But when you have seen vicious mobs lynch your mothers and fathers at will and drown your sisters and brothers at whim; when you have seen hate-filled policemen curse, kick and even kill your black brothers and sisters; when you see the vast majority of your twenty million Negro brothers smothering in an airtight cage of poverty in the midst of an affluent society; when you suddenly find your tongue twisted and your speech stammering as you seek to explain to your six-year-old daughter why she can't go to the public amusement park that has just been advertised on television, and see tears welling up in her eyes when she is told that Funtown is closed to colored children, and see ominous clouds of inferiority beginning to form in her little mental sky, and see her beginning to distort her personality by developing an unconscious bitterness toward white people; when you have to concoct an answer for a five-year-old son who is asking: "Daddy, why do white people treat colored people so mean?" When you take a cross-country drive and find it necessary to sleep night after night in the uncomfortable corners of your automobile because no motel will accept you; when you are humiliated day in and day out by nagging signs reading "white" and "colored"; when your first name becomes "nigger," your middle name becomes "boy" (however old you are) and your last name becomes "John," and your wife and mother are never given the respected title "Mrs."; when you are harried by day and haunted by night by the fact that you are a Negro, living constantly at tiptoe stance, never quite knowing what to expect next, and are plagued with inner fears and outer resentments; when you are forever fighting a degenerating sense of "nobodiness"—then you will understand why we find it difficult to wait. There comes a time when the cup of endurance runs over, and men are no longer willing to be plunged into the abyss of despair. I hope, sirs, you can understand our legitimate and unavoidable impatience.

You express a great deal of anxiety over our willingness to break laws. This is certainly a legitimate concern. Since we so diligently urge people to obey the Supreme Court's decision of 1954 outlawing segregation in the public schools, at first glance it may seem rather paradoxical for us consciously to break laws. One may well ask: "How can you advocate breaking some laws and obeying others?" The answer lies in the fact that there are two types of laws: just and unjust. I would be the first to advocate obeying just laws. One has not only a legal but a moral responsibility to obey just laws. Conversely, one has a moral responsibility to disobey unjust laws. I would agree with St. Augustine that "an unjust law is no law at all."

Now, what is the difference between the two? How does one determine whether a law is just or unjust? A just law is a man-made code that squares with the moral law or the law of God. An unjust law is a code that is out of harmony with the moral law. To put it in the terms of St. Thomas Aquinas: An unjust law is a human law that is not rooted in eternal law and natural law. Any law that uplifts human personality is just. Any law that degrades human personality is unjust. All segregation statutes are unjust because segregation distorts the soul and damages the personality. It gives the segregator a false sense of superiority and the segregated a false sense of inferiority. Segregation, to use the terminology of the Jewish philosopher Martin Buber, substitutes an "I—it" relationship for an "I—thou" relationship and ends up relegating persons to the status of things. Hence segregation is not only politically, economically and sociologically unsound, it is morally wrong and sinful. Paul Tillich has said that sin is separation. Is not segregation an existential expression of man's tragic separation, his awful estrangement, his terrible sinfulness? Thus it is that I can urge men to obey the 1954 decision of the Supreme Court, for it is morally right; and I can urge them to disobey segregation ordinances, for they are morally wrong.

Let us consider a more concrete example of just and unjust laws. An unjust law is a code that a numerical or power majority group compels a minority group to obey but does not make binding on itself. This is *difference* made legal. By the same token, a just law is a code that a majority compels a minority to follow and that it is willing to follow itself. This is *sameness* made legal.

Let me give another explanation. A law is unjust if it is inflicted on a minority that, as a result of being denied the right to vote, had no part in enacting or devising the law. Who can say that the legislature of Alabama which set up that state's segregation laws was democratically elected? Throughout Alabama all sorts of devious methods are used to prevent Negroes from becoming registered voters, and there are some counties in which, even though Negroes constitute a majority of the population, not a single Negro is registered. Can any law enacted under such circumstances be considered democratically structured?

Sometimes a law is just on its face and unjust in its application. For instance, I have been arrested on a charge of parading without a permit. Now, there is nothing wrong in having an ordinance which requires a permit for a parade. But such an ordinance becomes unjust when it is used to maintain segregation and to deny citizens the First-Amendment privilege of peaceful assembly and protest.

I hope you are able to see the distinction I am trying to point out. In no sense do I advocate evading or defying the law, as would the rabid segregationist. That would lead to anarchy. One who breaks an unjust law must do so openly, lovingly, and with a willingness to accept the penalty. I submit that an individual who breaks a law that conscience tells him is unjust, and who willingly accepts the penalty of imprisonment in order to arouse the conscience of the community over its injustice, is in reality expressing the highest respect for law.

Of course, there is nothing new about this kind of civil disobedience. It was evidenced sublimely in the refusal of Shadrach, Meshach and Abednego to obey the laws of Nebuchadnezzar, on the ground that a higher moral law was at stake. It was practiced superbly by the early Christians, who were willing to face hungry lions and the excruciating pain of chopping blocks rather than submit to certain unjust laws of the Roman Empire. To a degree, academic freedom is a reality today because Socrates practiced civil disobedience. In our own nation, the Boston Tea Party represented a massive act of civil disobedience.

We should never forget that everything Adolf Hitler did in Germany was "legal" and everything the Hungarian freedom fighters did in Hungary was "illegal." It was "illegal" to aid and comfort a Jew in Hitler's Germany. Even so, I am sure that, had I lived in Germany at the time, I would have aided and comforted my Jewish brothers. If today I lived in a Communist country where certain principles dear to the Christian faith are suppressed, I would openly advocate disobeying that country's antireligious laws.

I must make two honest confessions to you, my Christian and Jewish brothers. First, I must confess that over the past few years I have been gravely disappointed with the white moderate. I have almost reached the regrettable conclusion that the Negro's great stumbling block in his stride toward freedom is not the White Citizen's Counciler or the Ku Klux Klanner, but the white moderate, who is more devoted to "order" than to justice; who prefers a negative peace which is the absence of tension to a positive peace which is the presence of justice; who constantly says: "I agree with you in the goal you seek, but I cannot agree with your methods of direct action"; who paternalistically believes he can set the timetable for another man's freedom; who lives by a mythical concept of time and who constantly advises the Negro to wait for a "more convenient season." Shallow understanding from people of good will is more frustrating than absolute misunderstanding from people of ill will. Lukewarm acceptance is much more bewildering than outright rejection.

I had hoped that the white moderate would understand that law and order exist for the purpose of establishing justice and that when they fail in this purpose they become the dangerously structured dams that block the flow of social progress. I had hoped that the white moderate would understand that the present tension in the South is a necessary phase of the transition from an obnoxious negative peace, in which the Negro passively accepted his unjust plight, to a substantive and positive peace, in which all men will respect the dignity and worth of human personality. Actually, we who engage in nonviolent direct action are not the creators of tension. We merely bring to the surface the hidden tension that is already alive. We bring it out in the open, where it can be seen and dealt with. Like a boil that can never be cured so long as it is covered up but must be opened with all its ugliness to the natural medicines of air and light, injustice must be exposed, with all the tension its exposure creates, to the light of human conscience and the air of national opinion before it can be cured.

In your statement you assert that our actions, even though peaceful, must be condemned because they precipitate violence. But is this a logical assertion? Isn't this like condemning a robbed man because his possession of money precipitated the evil act of robbery? Isn't this like condemning Socrates because his unswerving commitment to truth and his philosophical inquiries precipitated the act by the misguided populace in which they made him drink hemlock? Isn't this like condemning Jesus because his unique God-consciousness and never-ceasing devotion to God's will precipitated the evil act of crucifixion? We must come to see that, as the federal courts have consistently affirmed, it is wrong to urge an individual to cease his efforts to gain his basic constitutional rights because the quest may precipitate violence. Society must protect the robbed and punish the robber.

I had also hoped that the white moderate would reject the myth concerning time in relation to the struggle for freedom. I have just received a letter from a white brother in Texas. He writes: "All Christians know that the colored people will receive equal rights eventually, but it is possible that you are in too great a religious hurry. It has taken Christianity almost two thousand years to accomplish what it has. The teachings of Christ take time to come to earth." Such an attitude stems from a tragic misconception of time, from the strangely irrational notion that there is something in the very flow of time that will inevitably cure all ills. Actually, time itself is neutral; it can be used either destructively or constructively. More and more I feel that the people of ill will have used time much more effectively than have the people of good will. We will have to repent in this generation not merely for the hateful words and actions of the bad people but for the appalling silence of the good people. Human progress never rolls in on wheels of inevitability; it comes through the tireless efforts of men willing to be co-workers with God, and without this hard work, time itself becomes an ally of the forces of social stagnation. We must use time creatively, in the knowledge that the time is always ripe to do right. Now is the time to make real the promise of democracy and transform our pending national elegy into a creative psalm of brotherhood. Now is the time to lift our national policy from the quicksand of racial injustice to the solid rock of human dignity.

You speak of our activity in Birmingham as extreme. At first I was rather disappointed that fellow clergymen would see my nonviolent efforts as those of an extremist. I began thinking about the fact that I stand in the middle of two opposing forces in the Negro community. One is a force of complacency, made up in part of Negroes who, as a result of long years of oppression, are so drained of self-respect and a sense of "somebodiness" that they have adjusted to segregation; and in part of a few middle-class Negroes who, because of a degree of academic and economic security and because in some ways they profit by segregation, have become insensitive to the problems of the masses. The other force is one of bitterness and hatred, and it comes perilously close to advocating violence. It is expressed in the various black nationalist groups that are springing up across the nation, the largest and best-known being Elijah Muhammad's Muslim movement. Nourished by the Negro's frustration over the continued existence of racial discrimination, this movement is made up of people who have lost faith in America, who have absolutely repudiated Christianity, and who have concluded that the white man is an incorrigible "devil."

I have tried to stand between these two forces, saying that we need emulate neither the "do-nothingism" of the complacent nor the hatred and despair of the black nationalist. For there is the more excellent way of love and nonviolent protest. I am grateful to God that, through the influence of the Negro church, the way of nonviolence became an integral part of our struggle.

If this philosophy had not emerged, by now many streets of

the South would, I am convinced, be flowing with blood. And I am further convinced that if our white brothers dismiss as "rabble-rousers" and "outside agitators" those of us who employ nonviolent direct action, and if they refuse to support our nonviolent efforts, millions of Negroes will, out of frustration and despair, seek solace and security in black-nationalist ideologies—a development that would inevitably lead to a frightening racial nightmare.

Oppressed people cannot remain oppressed forever. The yearning for freedom eventually manifests itself, and that is what has happened to the American Negro. Something within has reminded him of his birthright of freedom, and something without has reminded him that it can be gained. Consciously or unconsciously, he has been caught up by the *Zeitgeist*, and with his black brothers of Africa and his brown and yellow brothers of Asia, South America and the Caribbean, the United States Negro is moving with a sense of great urgency toward the promised land of racial justice. If one recognizes this vital urge that has engulfed the Negro community, one should readily understand why public demonstrations are taking place. The Negro has many pent-up resentments and latent frustrations, and he must release them. So let him march; let him make prayer pilgrimages to the city hall; let him go on freedom rides—and try to understand why he must do so. If his repressed emotions are not released in nonviolent ways, they will seek expression through violence; this is not a threat but a fact of history. So I have not said to my people: "Get rid of your discontent." Rather, I have tried to say that this normal and healthy discontent can be channeled into the creative outlet of nonviolent direct action. And now this approach is being termed extremist.

But though I was initially disappointed at being categorized as an extremist, as I continued to think about the matter I gradually gained a measure of satisfaction from the label. Was not Jesus an extremist for love? "Love your enemies, bless them that curse you, do good to them that hate you, and pray for them which despitefully use you, and persecute you." Was not

Amos an extremist for justice? "Let justice roll down like waters and righteousness like an ever-flowing stream." Was not Paul an extremist for the Christian gospel? "I bear in my body the marks of the Lord Jesus." Was not Martin Luther an extremist? "Here I stand; I cannot do otherwise, so help me God." And John Bunyan? "I will stay in jail to the end of my days before I make a butchery of my conscience." And Abraham Lincoln? "This nation cannot survive half slave and half free." And Thomas Jefferson? "We hold these truths to be self-evident, that all men are created equal . . ." So the question is not whether we will be extremists, but what kind of extremists we will be. Will we be extremists for hate or for love? Will we be extremists for the preservation of injustice or for the extension of justice? In that dramatic scene on Calvary's hill three men were crucified. We must never forget that all three were crucified for the same crime—the crime of extremism. Two were extremists for immorality, and thus fell below their environment. The other, Jesus Christ, was an extremist for love, truth and goodness, and thereby rose above his environment. Perhaps the South, the nation and the world are in dire need of creative extremists.

I had hoped that the white moderate would see this need. Perhaps I was too optimistic; perhaps I expected too much. I suppose I should have realized that few members of the oppressor race can understand the deep groans and passionate yearnings of the oppressed race, and still fewer have the vision to see that injustice must be rooted out by strong, persistent and determined action. I am thankful, however, that some of our white brothers in the South have grasped the meaning of this social revolution and committed themselves to it. They are still all too few in quantity, but they are big in quality. Some—such as Ralph McGill, Lillian Smith, Harry Golden, James McBride Dabbs, Ann Braden and Sarah Patton Boyle—have written about our struggle in eloquent and prophetic terms. Others have marched with us down nameless streets of the South. They have languished in filthy, roach-infested jails, suffering the abuse and brutality of policemen who view them as "dirty nigger-lovers." Unlike so many of their moderate brothers and sisters, they have recognized the urgency of the moment and sensed the need for powerful "action" antidotes to combat the disease of segregation.

Let me take note of my other major disappointment. I have been so greatly disappointed with the white church and its leadership. Of course, there are some notable exceptions. I am not unmindful of the fact that each of you has taken some significant stands on this issue. I commend you, Reverend Stallings, for your Christian stand on this past Sunday, in welcoming Negroes to your worship service on a nonsegregated basis. I commend the Catholic leaders of this state for integrating Spring Hill College several years ago.

But despite these notable exceptions, I must honestly reiterate that I have been disappointed with the church. I do not say this as one of those negative critics who can always find something wrong with the church. I say this as a minister of the gospel, who loves the church; who was nurtured in its bosom; who has been sustained by its spiritual blessings and who will remain true to it as long as the cord of life shall lengthen.

When I was suddenly catapulted into the leadership of the bus protest in Montgomery, Alabama, a few years ago, I felt we would be supported by the white church. I felt that the white ministers, priests and rabbis of the South would be among our strongest allies. Instead, some have been outright opponents, refusing to understand the freedom movement and misrepresenting its leaders; all too many others have been more cautious than courageous and have remained silent behind the anesthetizing security of stained-glass windows.

In spite of my shattered dreams, I came to Birmingham with the hope that the white religious leadership of this community would see the justice of our cause and, with deep moral concern, would serve as the channel through which our just grievances could reach the power structure. I had hoped that each of you would understand. But again I have been disappointed.

I have heard numerous southern religious leaders admonish their worshipers to comply with a desegregation decision because it is the law, but I have longed to hear white ministers declare: "Follow this decree because integration is morally right and because the Negro is your brother." In the midst of blatant injustices inflicted upon the Negro, I have watched white churchmen stand on the sideline and mouth pious irrelevancies and sanctimonious trivialities. In the midst of a mighty struggle to rid our nation of racial and economic injustice, I have heard many ministers say: "Those are social issues, with which the gospel has no real concern." And I have watched many churches commit themselves to a completely otherworldly religion which makes a strange, unbiblical distinction between body and soul, between the sacred and the secular.

I have traveled the length and breadth of Alabama, Mississippi and all the other southern states. On sweltering summer days and crisp autumn mornings I have looked at the South's beautiful churches with their lofty spires pointing heavenward. I have beheld the impressive outlines of her massive religious-education buildings. Over and over I have found myself asking: "What kind of people worship here? Who is their God? Where were their voices when the lips of Governor Barnett dripped with words of interposition and nullification? Where were they when Governor Wallace gave a clarion call for defiance and hatred? Where were their voices of support when bruised and weary Negro men and women decided to rise from the dark dungeons of complacency to the bright hills of creative protest?"

Yes, these questions are still in my mind. In deep disappointment I have wept over the laxity of the church. But be assured that my tears have been tears of love. There can be no deep disappointment where there is not deep love. Yes, I love the church. How could I do otherwise? I am in the rather unique position of being the son, the grandson and the great-grandson of preachers. Yes, I see the church as the body of Chirst. But, oh! How we have blemished and scarred that body through social neglect and through fear of being nonconformists.

There was a time when the church was very powerful—in the time when the early Christians rejoiced at being deemed worthy to suffer for what they believed. In those days the church was not merely a thermometer that recorded the ideas and principles of popular opinion; it was a thermostat that transformed the mores of society. Whenever the early Christians entered a town, the people in power became disturbed and immediately sought to convict the Christians for being "disturbers of the peace" and "outside agitators." But the Christians pressed on, in the conviction that they were "a colony of heaven," called to obey God rather than man. Small in number, they were big in commitment. They were too God-intoxicated to be "astronomically intimidated." By their effort and example they brought an end to such ancient evils as infanticide and gladiatorial contests.

Things are different now. So often the contemporary church is a weak, ineffectual voice with an uncertain sound. So often it is an archdefender of the status quo. Far from being disturbed by the presence of the church, the power structure of the average community is consoled by the church's silent—and often even vocal—sanction of things as they are.

But the judgment of God is upon the church as never before. If today's church does not recapture the sacrificial spirit of the early church, it will lose its authenticity, forfeit the loyalty of millions, and be dismissed as an irrelevant social club with no meaning for the twentieth century. Every day I meet young people whose disappointment with the church has turned into outright disgust.

Perhaps I have once again been too optimistic. Is organized religion too inextricably bound to the status quo to save our nation and the world? Perhaps I must turn my faith to the inner spiritual church, the church within the church, as the true *ekklesia* and the hope of the world. But again I am thankful to God that some noble souls from the ranks of organized religion have broken loose from the paralyzing chains of conformity and joined us as active partners in the struggle for freedom. They have left their secure congregations and walked the streets of Albany, Georgia, with us. They have gone down the highways of the South on tortuous rides for freedom. Yes, they have gone to jail with us. Some have been dismissed from their churches, have lost the support of their bishops and fellow ministers. But they have acted in the faith that right defeated is stronger than evil triumphant. Their witness has been the spiritual salt that has preserved the true meaning of the gospel in these troubled times. They have carved a tunnel of hope through the dark mountain of disappointment.

I hope the church as a whole will meet the challenge of this decisive hour. But even if the church does not come to the aid of justice, I have no despair about the future. I have no fear about the outcome of our struggle in Birmingham, even if our motives are at present misunderstood. We will reach the goal of freedom in Birmingham and all over the nation, because the goal of America is freedom. Abused and scorned though we may be, our destiny is tied up with America's destiny. Before the pilgrims landed at Plymouth, we were here. Before the pen of Jefferson etched the majestic words of the Declaration of Independence across the pages of history, we were here. For more than two centuries our forebears labored in this country without wages; they made cotton king; they built the homes of their masters while suffering gross injustice and shameful humiliation—and yet out of a bottomless vitality they continued to thrive and develop. If the inexpressible cruelties of slavery could not stop us, the opposition we now face will surely fail. We will win our freedom because the sacred heritage of our nation and the eternal will of God are embodied in our echoing demands.

Before closing I feel impelled to mention one other point in your statement that has troubled me profoundly. You warmly commended the Birmingham police force for keeping "order" and "preventing violence." I doubt that you would have so warmly commended the police force if you had seen its dogs sinking their teeth into unarmed, nonviolent Negroes. I doubt that you would so quickly commend the policemen if you were to observe their ugly and inhumane treatment of Negroes here in the city jail; if you were to watch them push and curse old Negro women and young Negro girls; if you were to see them slap and kick old Negro men and young boys; if you were to observe them, as they did on two occasions, refuse to give us food because we wanted to sing our grace together. I cannot join you in your praise of the Birmingham police department.

It is true that the police have exercised a degree of discipline in handling the demonstrators. In this sense they have conducted themselves rather "nonviolently" in public. But for what purpose? To preserve the evil system of segregation. Over the past few years I have consistently preached that nonviolence demands that the means we use must be as pure as the ends we seek. I have tried to make clear that it is wrong to use immoral means to attain moral ends. But now I must affirm that it is just as wrong, or perhaps even more so, to use moral means to preserve immoral ends. Perhaps Mr. Connor and his policemen have been rather nonviolent in public, as was Chief Pritchett in Albany, Georgia, but they have used the moral means of nonviolence to maintain the immoral end of racial injustice. As T. S. Eliot has said: "The last temptation is the greatest treason: To do the right deed for the wrong reason."

I wish you had commended the Negro sit-inners and demonstrators of Birmingham for their sublime courage, their willingness to suffer and their amazing discipline in the midst of great provocation. One day the South will recognize its real heroes. They will be the James Merediths, with the noble sense of purpose that enables them to face jeering and hostile mobs, and with the agonizing loneliness that characterizes the life of the pioneer. They will be old, oppressed, battered Negro women, symbolized in a seventy-two-year-old woman in Montgomery, Alabama, who rose up with a sense of dignity and with her people decided not to ride segregated buses, and who responded with ungrammatical profundity to one who inquired about her weariness: "My feets is tired, but my soul is at rest." They will be the young high school and college students, the young ministers of the gospel and a host of their elders, courageously and nonviolently sitting in at lunch counters and willingly going to jail for conscience's sake. One day the South will know that when these disinherited children of God sat down at lunch counters, they were in reality standing up for what is best in the American dream and for the most sacred values in our Judaeo-Christian heritage, thereby bringing our nation back to those great wells of democracy which were dug deep by the founding fathers in their formulation of the Constitution and the Declaration of Independence.

Never before have I written so long a letter. I'm afraid it is much too long to take your precious time. I can assure you that it would have been much shorter if I had been writing from a comfortable desk, but what else can one do when he is alone in a narrow jail cell, other than write long letters, think long thoughts and pray long prayers?

If I have said anything in this letter that overstates the truth and indicates an unreasonable impatience, I beg you to forgive me. If I have said anything that understates the truth and indicates my having a patience that allows me to settle for anything less than brotherhood, I beg God to forgive me.

I hope this letter finds you strong in the faith. I also hope that circumstances will soon make it possible for me to meet each of you, not as an integrationist or a civil-rights leader but as a fellow clergyman and a Christian brother. Let us all hope that the dark clouds of racial prejudice will soon pass away and the deep fog of misunderstanding will be lifted from our fear-drenched communities, and in some not too distant tomorrow the radiant stars of love and brotherhood will shine over our great nation with all their scintillating beauty.

Yours for the cause of Peace and Brotherhood,
Martin Luther King, Jr.

14. MALCOLM X

The Ballot or the Bullet

(1964)

MALCOLM X's "The Ballot or the Bullet" is recognized as one of the most powerful speeches in American history. Born Malcolm Little, Malcolm X (1925–1965) grew up in Michigan and was a hustler and a con artist in Boston before he was arrested for robbery in 1946. While in prison, Malcolm converted to the Nation of Islam (NOI) and changed his name to Malcolm X. Following his release, he quickly became the NOI's most prominent minister. However, he was suspended from the NOI for a controversial remark he made after the assassination of President John F. Kennedy. In 1964, Malcolm left the NOI, traveled to Mecca, and established the Organization of Afro-American Unity. In his last year, Malcolm retreated somewhat from his previously held belief that whites were "devils," and he began to embrace an internationalist socialist philosophy of black liberation. He was assassinated in the Audubon Ballroom in Harlem, New York, in 1965. "The Ballot or the Bullet" was delivered in Cleveland, Ohio, on April 3, 1964. By refusing to repudiate nonviolence, Malcolm recognized that he made Martin Luther King, Jr.'s, stance seem more moderate and palatable than it would otherwise have appeared.

SOURCE: George Breitman, ed., *Malcolm X Speaks: Selected Speeches and Statements*. New York: Merit Publishers, 1965.

SELECTED READINGS: Michael Eric Dyson, *The Myth and Meaning of Malcolm X* (1995). James Cone, *Martin and Malcolm: A Dream or a Nightmare?* (1991). George Breitman, *The Last Year of Malcolm X* (1967).

Mr. Moderator, brothers and sisters, friends and enemies: I just can't believe everyone in here is a friend and I don't want to leave anybody out. The question tonight, as I understand it, is "The Negro Revolt, and Where Do We Go from Here?" or "What Next?" In my little humble way of understanding it, it points toward either the ballot or the bullet. . . .

Before we try and explain what is meant by the ballot or the bullet, I would like to clarify something concerning myself. I'm still a Muslim, my religion is still Islam. That's my personal belief. Just as Adam Clayton Powell is a Christian minister who heads the Abyssinian Baptist Church in New York, but at the same time takes part in the political struggles to try and bring about rights to the black people in this country; and Dr. Martin Luther King is a Christian minister down in Atlanta, Georgia, who heads another organization fighting for the civil rights of black people in this country; and Reverend Galamison—I guess you've heard of him—is another Christian minister in New York who has been deeply involved in the school boycotts to eliminate segregated education; well, I myself am a minister, not a Christian minister, but a Muslim minister; and I believe in action on all fronts by whatever means necessary.

Although I'm still a Muslim, I'm not here tonight to discuss my religion. I'm not here to try and change your religion. I'm not here to argue or discuss anything that we differ about, because it's time for us to submerge our differences and realize that it is best for us to first see that we have the same problem, a common problem—a problem that will make you catch hell whether you're a Baptist, or a Methodist, or a Muslim, or a nationalist. Whether you're educated or illiterate, whether you live on the boulevard or in the alley, you're going to catch hell just like I am. We're all in the same boat and we all are going to catch the same hell from the same man. He just happens to be a white man. All of us have suffered here, in this country, political oppression at the hands of the white man, economic exploitation at at the hands of the white man, and social degradation at the hands of the white man.

Now in speaking like this, it doesn't mean that we're anti-white, but it does mean we're anti-exploitation, we're anti-degradation, we're anti-oppression. And if the white man doesn't want us to be anti-*him*, let him stop oppressing and exploiting and degrading us. Whether we are Christians or Muslims or nationalists or agnostics or atheists, we must first learn to forget our differences. If we have differences, let us differ in the closet; when we come out in front, let us not have anything to argue about until we get finished arguing with the man. If the late President Kennedy could get together with Khrushchev and exchange some wheat, we certainly have more in common with each other than Kennedy and Khrushchev had with each other.

If we don't do something real soon, I think you'll have to agree that we're going to be forced either to use the ballot or the bullet. It's one or the other in 1964. It isn't that time is running out—time has run out! Nineteen sixty-four threatens to be the most explosive year America has ever witnessed. The most explosive year. Why? It's also a political year. It's the year when all of the white politicians will be back in the so-called Negro community jiving you and me for some votes. The year when all of the white political crooks will be right back in your and my community with their false promises, building up our hopes for a letdown, with their trickery and their treachery, with their false promises which they don't intend to keep. As they nourish these dissatisfactions, it can only lead to one thing, an explosion; and now we have the type of black man on the scene in America today—I'm sorry, Brother Lomax—who just doesn't intend to turn the other cheek any longer.

Don't let anybody tell you anything about the odds are against you. If they draft you, they send you to Korea and make you face 800 million Chinese. If you can be brave over there, you can be brave right here. These odds aren't as great as those odds. And if you fight here, you will at least know what you're fighting for.

I'm not a politician, not even a student of politics; in fact, I'm not a student of much of anything. I'm not a Democrat, I'm not a Republican, and I don't even consider myself an American. If you and I were Americans, there'd be no problem. Those Hunkies that just got off the boat, they're already Americans; Polacks are already Americans; the Italian refugees are already Americans. Everything that came out of Europe, every blue-eyed thing, is already an American. And as long as you and I have been over here, we aren't Americans yet.

Well, I am one who doesn't believe in deluding myself. I'm not going to sit at your table and watch you eat, with nothing on my plate, and call myself a diner. Sitting at the table doesn't make you a diner, unless you eat some of what's on that plate. Being here in America doesn't make you an American. Being born here in America doesn't make you an American. Why, if birth made you American, you wouldn't need any legislation, you wouldn't need any amendments to the Constitution, you wouldn't be faced with civil-rights filibustering in Washington, D.C., right now. They don't have to pass civil-rights legislation to make a Polack an American.

No, I'm not an American. I'm one of the twenty-two million black people who are the victims of democracy, nothing but disguised hypocrisy. So, I'm not standing here speaking to you as an American, or a patriot, or a flag-saluter, or a flag-waver—no, not I. I'm speaking as a victim of this American system. And I see America through the eyes of the victim. I don't see any American dream; I see an American nightmare.

These twenty-two million victims are waking up. Their eyes are coming open. They're beginning to see what they used to only look at. They're becoming politically mature. They are realizing that there are new political trends from coast to coast. . . .

So it's time in 1964 to wake up. And when you see them coming up with that kind of conspiracy, let them know your eyes are open. And let them know you got something else that's wide open too. It's got to be the ballot or the bullet. The ballot or the bullet. If you're afraid to use an expression like that, you should get on out of the country, you should get back in the cotton patch, you should get back in the alley. They get all the Negro vote, and after they get it, the Negro gets nothing in return. All they did when they got to Washington was give a few big Negroes big jobs. Those big Negroes didn't need big jobs, they already had jobs. That's camouflage, that's trickery, that's treachery, window-dressing. I'm not trying to knock out the Democrats for the Republicans, we'll get to them in a minute. But it is true—you put the Democrats first and the Democrats put you last.

Look at it the way it is. What alibis do they use, since they control Congress and the Senate? What alibi do they use when you and I ask, "Well, when are you going to keep your promise?" They blame the Dixiecrats. What is a Dixiecrat? A Democrat. A Dixiecrat is nothing but a Democrat in disguise. The titular head of the Democrats is also the head of the Dixiecrats, because the Dixiecrats are a party of the Democratic Party. The Democrats have never kicked the Dixiecrats out of the party. The Dixiecrats bolted themselves once, but the Democrats didn't put them out. Imagine, these low-down Southern segregationists put the Northern Democrats down. But the Northern Democrats have never put the Dixiecrats down. No, look at that thing the way it is. They have got a con game going on, a political con game, and you and I are in the middle. It's time for you and me to wake up and start looking at it like it is, and trying to understand it like it is; and then we can deal with it like it is. . . .

So, what I'm trying to impress upon you, in essence, is this: You and I in America are faced not with a segregationist conspiracy, we're faced with a government conspiracy. Everyone who's filibustering is a Senator—that's the government. Everyone who's finagling in Washington, D.C., is a Congressman—that's the government. You don't have anybody putting blocks in your path but people who are a part of the government. The same government that you go abroad to fight for and die for is the government that is in a conspiracy to deprive you of your voting rights, deprive you of your economic opportunities, deprive you of decent housing, deprive you of decent education. You don't need to go to the employer alone, it is the government itself, the government of America, that is responsible for the oppression and exploitation and degradation of black people in this country. And you should drop it in their lap. This government has failed the Negro. This so-called democracy has failed the Negro. And all these white liberals have definitely failed the Negro.

So, where do we go from here? First, we need some friends. We need some new allies. The entire civil-rights struggle needs a new interpretation, a broader interpretation. We need to look at this civil-rights thing from another angle—from the inside as well as from the outside. To those of us whose philosophy is black nationalism, the only way you can get involved in the civil-rights struggle is to give it a new interpretation. That old interpretation excluded us. It kept us out. So, we're giving a new interpretation to the civil-rights struggle, an interpretation that will enable us to come into it, take part in it. And these handkerchief-heads who have been dillydallying and pussyfooting and compromising—we don't intend to let them pussyfoot and dillydally and compromise any longer.

How can you thank a man for giving you what's already yours? How then can you thank him for giving you only part of what's already yours? You haven't even made progress, if what's being given to you, you should have had already. That's not progress. And I love my Brother Lomax, the way he pointed out we're right back where we were in 1954. We're not even as far up as we were in 1954. We're behind where we were in 1954. There's more segregation now than there was in 1954. There's more racial animosity, more racial hatred, more racial violence today, in 1964, than there was in 1954. Where is the progress?

And now you're facing a situation where the young Negro's coming up. They don't want to hear that "turn-the-other-cheek" stuff, no. In Jacksonville, those were teenagers, they were throwing Molotov cocktails. Negroes have never done that before. But it shows you there's a new deal coming in. There's new thinking coming in. There's new strategy coming in. It'll be Molotov cocktails this month, hand grenades next month, and something else next month. It'll be ballots, or it'll be bullets. It'll be liberty, or it will be death. The only difference about this kind of death—it'll be reciprocal. You know what is meant by "reciprocal"? That's one of Brother Lomax's words, I stole it from him. I don't usually deal with those big words because I don't usually deal with big people. I deal with small people. I find you can get a whole lot of small people and whip hell out of a whole lot of big people. They haven't got anything to lose, and they've got everything to gain. And they'll let you know in a minute: "It takes two to tango; when I go, you go."

The black nationalists, those whose philosophy is black nationalism, in bringing about this new interpretation of the entire meaning of civil rights, look upon it as meaning, as Brother Lomax has pointed out, equality of opportunity. Well, we're justified in seeking civil rights, if it means equality of opportunity, because all we're doing there is trying to collect for our investment. Our mothers and fathers invested sweat and blood. Three hundred and ten years we worked in this country without a dime in return—I mean without a *dime* in return. You let the white man walk around here talking about how rich this country is, but you never stop to think how it got rich so quick. It got rich because you made it rich.

You take the people who are in this audience right now. They're poor, we're all poor as individuals. Our weekly salary individually amounts to hardly anything. But if you take the salary of everyone in here collectively it'll fill up a whole lot of baskets. It's a lot of wealth. If you can collect the wages of just these people right here for a year, you'll be rich—richer than rich. When you look at it like that, think how rich Uncle Sam had to become, not with this handful, but millions of black people. Your and my mother and father, who didn't work an eight-hour shift, but worked from "can't see" in the morning until "can't see" at night, and worked for nothing, making the white man rich, making Uncle Sam rich. . . .

By ballot I only mean freedom. Don't you know—I disagree with Lomax on this issue—that the ballot is more important than the dollar? Can I prove it? Yes. Look in the U.N. There are poor nations in the U.N.; yet those poor nations can get together with their voting power and keep the rich nations from making a move. They have one nation, one vote—everyone has an equal vote. And when those brothers from Asia, and Africa and the darker parts of this earth get together, their voting power is sufficient to hold Sam in check. Or Russia in check. Or some other section of the earth in check. So, the ballot is most important.

Right now, in this country, if you and I, twenty-two million African-Americans—that's what we are—Africans who are in

America. In fact, you'd get farther calling yourself African instead of Negro. Africans don't catch hell. You're the only one catching hell. They don't have to pass civil-rights bills for Africans. An African can go anywhere he wants right now. All you've got to do is tie your head up. That's right, go anywhere you want. Just stop being a Negro. Change your name to Hoogagagooba. That'll show you how silly the white man is. You're dealing with a silly man. A friend of mine who's very dark put a turban on his head and went into a restaurant in Atlanta before they called themselves desegregated. He went into a white restaurant, he sat down, they served him, and he said, "What would happen if a Negro came in here?" And there he's sitting, black as night, but because he had his head wrapped up the waitress looked back at him and says, "Why, there wouldn't no nigger dare come in here."

So, you're dealing with a man whose bias and prejudice are making him lose his mind, his intelligence, every day. He's frightened. He looks around and sees what's taking place on this earth, and he sees that the pendulum of time is swinging in your direction. The dark people are waking up. They're losing their fear of the white man. No place where he's fighting right now is he winning. Everywhere he's fighting, he's fighting someone your and my complexion. And they're beating him. He can't win any more. He's won his last battle. He failed to win the Korean War. He couldn't win it. He had to sign a truce. That's a loss. Any time Uncle Sam, with all his machinery for warfare, is held to a draw by some rice-eaters, he's lost the battle. He had to sign a truce. America's not supposed to sign a truce. She's supposed to be bad. But she's not bad any more. She's bad as long as she can use her hydrogen bomb, but she can't use hers for fear Russia might use hers. Russia can't use hers, for fear that Sam might use his. So, both of them are weaponless. They can't use the weapon, because each's weapon nullifies the other's. So the only place where action can take place is on the ground. And the white man can't win another war fighting on the ground. Those days are over. The black man knows it, the brown man knows it, the red man knows it, and the yellow man knows it. So they engage him in guerrilla warfare. That's not his style. You've got to have heart to be a guerrilla warrior, and he hasn't got any heart. I'm telling you now. . . .

It's time for you and me to stop sitting in this country, letting some cracker Senators, Northern crackers and Southern crackers, sit there in Washington, D.C., and come to a conclusion in their mind that you and I are supposed to have civil rights. There's no white man going to tell me anything about *my* rights. Brothers and sisters, always remember, if it doesn't take Senators and Congressmen and Presidential proclamations to give freedom to the white man, it is not necessary for legislation or proclamation or Supreme Court decisions to give freedom to the black man. You let that white man know, if this is a country of freedom, let it be a country of freedom; and if it's not a country of freedom, change it. . . .

Last but not least, I must say this concerning the great controversy over rifles and shotguns. The only thing that I've ever said is that in areas where the government has proven itself either unwilling or unable to defend the lives and the property of Negroes, it's time for Negroes to defend themselves. Article number two of the Constitutional amendments provides you and me the right to own a rifle or a shotgun. It is constitutionally legal to own a shotgun or a rifle. This doesn't mean you're going to get a rifle and form battalions and go out looking for white folks, although you'd be within your rights—I mean, you'd be justified; but that would be illegal and we don't do anything illegal. If the white man doesn't want the black man buying rifles and shotguns, then let the government do its job. That's all. And don't let the white man come to you and ask you what you think about what Malcolm says—why, you old Uncle Tom. He would never ask you if he thought you were going to say, "Oh, man!" No, he is making a Tom out of you.

So, this doesn't mean forming rifle clubs and going out looking for people, but it is time, in 1964, if you are a man, to let that man know. If he's not going to do his job in running the government and providing you and me with the protection that our taxes are supposed to be for, since he spends all those billions for his defense budget, he certainly can't begrudge you and me spending $12 or $15 for a single-shot, or double-action. I hope you understand. Don't go out shooting people, but any time, brothers and sisters, and especially the men in this audience—some of you wearing Congressional Medals of Honor, with shoulders this wide, chests this big, muscles that big—any time you and I sit around and read where they bomb a church and murder in cold blood, not some grownups, but four little girls while they were praying . . . if you never see me another time in your life, if I die in the morning, I'll die saying one thing: the ballot or the bullet, the ballot or the bullet.

If a Negro in 1964 has to sit around and wait for some cracker Senator to filibuster when it comes to the rights of black people, why, you and I should hang our heads in shame. You talk about a march on Washington in 1963, you haven't seen anything. There's some more going down in '64. And this time they're not going like they went last year. They're not going singing "We Shall Overcome." They're not going with white friends. They're not going with placards already painted for them. They're not going with round-trip tickets. They're going with one-way tickets.

And if they don't want that non-nonviolent army going down there, tell them to bring the filibuster to a halt. The black nationalists aren't going to wait. Lyndon B. Johnson is the head of the Democratic party. If he's for civil rights, let him go into the Senate next week and declare himself. Let him go in there right now and declare himself. Let him go in there and denounce the Southern branch of his party. Let him go in there right now and take a moral stand—right now, not later. Tell him, don't wait until election time. If he waits too long, brothers and sisters, he will be responsible for letting a condition develop in this country which will create a climate that will bring seeds up out of the ground with vegetation on the end of them looking like something these people never dreamed of. In 1964, it's the ballot or the bullet. Thank you.

15. HERBERT MARCUSE

One Dimensional Man
(1964)

HERBERT MARCUSE's *One Dimensional Man* is often credited with supplying a rationale for the youth revolt of the 1960s, and Marcuse was one of the New Left's foremost intellectual defenders. Born in Berlin, Marcuse (1898–1979) came to the United States in 1934 to escape Nazism. In 1940 he became a naturalized U.S. citizen. He taught at numerous American universities and made enduring contributions as a philosopher and social theorist of revolutionary change, drawing on the works of Marx and Freud in his effort to formulate a comprehensive critique of advanced industrial society. In his most famous work, *One Dimensional Man*, he argued that individuals were being sapped of their ability for critical thinking and oppositional behavior as they fell under the sway of existing patterns of production and consumption.

SOURCE: Herbert Marcuse. *One Dimensional Man: Studies in the Ideology of Advanced Industrial Society.* Boston: Beacon Press, 1964.

SELECTED READINGS: Barry Katz, *Herbert Marcuse and the Art of Liberation: An Intellectual Biography* (1982). Douglas Kellner, *Herbert Marcuse and the Crisis of Marxism* (1984). Morton Schoolman, *Imaginary Witness: The Critical Theory of Herbert Marcuse* (1984).

The Paralysis of Criticism:
Society Without Opposition

Does not the threat of an atomic catastrophe which could wipe out the human race also serve to protect the very forces which perpetuate this danger? The efforts to prevent such a catastrophe overshadow the search for its potential causes in contemporary industrial society. These causes remain unidentified, unexposed, unattacked by the public because they recede before the all too obvious threat from without—to the West from the East, to the East from the West. Equally obvious is the need for being prepared, for living on the brink, for facing the challenge. We submit to the peaceful production of the means of destruction, to the perfection of waste, to being educated for a defense which deforms the defenders and that which they defend.

If we attempt to relate the causes of the danger to the way in which society is organized and organizes its members, we are immediately confronted with the fact that advanced industrial society becomes richer, bigger, and better as it perpetuates the danger. The defense structure makes life easier for a greater number of people and extends man's mastery of nature. Under these circumstances, our mass media have little difficulty in selling particular interests as those of all sensible men. The political needs of society become individual needs and aspirations, their satisfaction promotes business and the commonweal, and the whole appears to be the very embodiment of Reason.

And yet this society is irrational as a whole. Its productivity is destructive of the free development of human needs and faculties, its peace maintained by the constant threat of war, its growth dependent on the repression of the real possibilities for pacifying the struggle for existence—individual, national, and international. This repression, so different from that which characterized the preceding, less developed stages of our society, operates today not from a position of natural and technical immaturity but rather from a position of strength. The capabilities (intellectual and material) of contemporary society are immeasurably greater than ever before—which means that the scope of society's domination over the individual is immeasurably greater than ever before. Our society distinguishes itself by conquering the centrifugal social forces with Technology rather than Terror, on the dual basis of an overwhelming efficiency and an increasing standard of living.

To investigate the roots of these developments and examine their historical alternatives is part of the aim of a critical theory of contemporary society, a theory which analyzes society in the light of its used and unused or abused capabilities for improving the human condition. But what are the standards for such a critique?

Certainly value judgments play a part. The established way of organizing society is measured against other possible ways, ways which are held to offer better chances for alleviating man's struggle for existence; a specific historical practice is measured against its own historical alternatives. From the beginning, any critical theory of society is thus confronted with the problem of historical objectivity, a problem which arises at the two points where the analysis implies value judgments:

1. The judgment that human life is worth living, or rather can be and ought to be made worth living. This judgment underlies all intellectual effort; it is the *a priori* of social theory, and its rejection (which is perfectly logical) rejects theory itself;

2. The judgment that, in a given society, specific possibilities exist for the amelioration of human life and specific ways and means of realizing these possibilities. Critical analysis has to demonstrate the objective validity of these judgments, and the demonstration has to proceed on empirical grounds. The established society has available an ascertainable quantity and quality of intellectual and material resources. How can these resources be used for the optimal development and satisfaction of individual needs and faculties with a minimum of toil and misery? Social theory is historical theory, and history is the realm of chance in the realm of necessity. Therefore, among the various possible and actual modes of organizing and utilizing the available resources, which ones offer the greatest chance of an optimal development?

The attempt to answer these questions demands a series of initial abstractions. In order to identify and define the possibilities of an optimal development, the critical theory must abstract from the actual organization and utilization of society's resources, and from the results of this organization and utilization. Such abstraction, which refuses to accept the given universe of facts as the final context of validation, such "transcending" analysis of the facts in the light of their arrested and denied possibilities, pertains to the very structure of social theory. It is opposed to all metaphysics by virtue of the rigorously historical character of the transcendence.* The "possibilities" must be within the reach of the respective society; they must be definable goals of practice. By the same token, the abstraction from the established institutions must be expressive of an actual tendency—that is, their transformation must be the real need of the underlying population. Social theory is concerned with the historical alternatives which haunt the established society as subversive tendencies and forces. The values attached to the alternatives do become facts when they are translated into reality by historical practice. The theoretical concepts terminate with social change.

But here, advanced industrial society confronts the critique with a situation which seems to deprive it of its very basis. Technical progress, extended to a whole system of domination and coordination, creates forms of life (and of power) which appear to reconcile the forces opposing the system and to defeat or refute all protest in the name of the historical prospects of freedom from toil and domination. Contemporary society seems to be capable of containing social change—qualitative change which would establish essentially different institutions, a new direction of the productive process, new modes of human existence. This containment of social change is perhaps the most singular achievement of advanced industrial society; the general acceptance of the National Purpose, bipartisan policy, the decline of pluralism, the collusion of Business and Labor within the strong State testify to the integration of opposites which is the result as well as the prerequisite of this achievement.

A brief comparison between the formative stage of the theory of industrial society and its present situation may help to show how the

---

*The terms "transcend" and "transcendence" are used throughout in the empirical, critical sense: they designate tendencies in theory and practice which, in a given society, "overshoot" the established universe or discourse and action toward its historical alternatives (real possibilities).

basis of the critique has been altered. At its origins in the first half of the nineteenth century, when it elaborated the first concepts of the alternatives, the critique of industrial society attained concreteness in a historical mediation between theory and practice, values and facts, needs and goals. This historical mediation occurred in the conscious-ness and in the political action of the two great classes which faced each other in the society: the bourgeoisie and the proletariat. In the capitalist world, they are still the basic classes. However, the capitalist development has altered the structure and function of these two classes in such a way that they no longer appear to be agents of his-torical transformation. An overriding interest in the preservation and improvement of the institutional status quo unites the former antago-nists in the most advanced areas of contemporary society. And to the degree to which technical progress assures the growth and cohesion of communist society, the very idea of qualitative change recedes be-fore the realistic notions of a non-explosive evolution. In the absence of demonstrable agents and agencies of social change, the critique is thus thrown back to a high level of abstraction. There is no ground on which theory and practice, thought and action meet. Even the most empirical analysis of historical alternatives appears to be unrealistic speculation, and commitment to them a matter of personal (or group) preference.

And yet: does this absence refute the theory? In the face of appar-ently contradictory facts, the critical analysis continues to insist that the need for qualitative change is as pressing as ever before. Needed by whom? The answer continues to be the same: by the society as a whole, for every one of its members. The union of growing productiv-ity and growing destruction; the brinkmanship of annihilation; the surrender of thought, hope, and fear to the decisions of the powers that be; the preservation of misery in the face of unprecedented wealth constitute the most impartial indictment—even if they are not the *raison d'être* of this society but only its by-product: its sweeping ratio-nality, which propels efficiency and growth, is itself irrational.

The fact that the vast majority of the population accepts, and is made to accept, this society does not render it less irrational and less reprehensible. The distinction between true and false consciousness, real and immediate interest, still is meaningful. But this distinction itself must be validated. Men must come to see it and to find their way from false to true consciousness, from their immediate to their real interest. They can do so only if they live in need of changing their way of life, of denying the positive, of refusing. It is precisely this need which the established society manages to repress to the degree to which it is capable of "delivering the goods" on an increasingly large scale, and using the scientific conquest of nature for the scientific conquest of man.

Confronted with the total character of the achievements of advanced industrial society, critical theory is left without the rationale for transcending this society. The vacuum empties the theoretical structure itself, because the categories of a critical social theory were developed during the period in which the need for refusal and subversion was embodied in the action of effective social forces. These categories were essentially negative and oppositional concepts, defining the actual contradictions in nineteenth-century European society. The category "society" itself expressed the acute conflict between the social and political sphere—society as antagonistic to the state. Similarly, "individual," "class," "private," "family" denoted spheres and forces not yet integrated with the established conditions—spheres of tension and contradiction. With the growing integration of industrial society, these categories are losing their critical connotation, and tend to become descriptive, deceptive, or operational terms.

An attempt to recapture the critical intent of these categories, and to understand how the intent was cancelled by the social reality, appears from the outset to be regression from a theory joined with historical practice to abstract, speculative thought: from the critique of political economy to philosophy. This ideological character of the critique results from the fact that the analysis is forced to proceed from a position "outside" the positive as well as negative, the productive as well as destructive tendencies in society. Modern industrial society is the pervasive identity of these opposites—it is the whole that is in question. At the same time, the position of theory cannot be one of mere speculation. It must be a historical position in the sense that it must be grounded on the capabilities of the given society.

This ambiguous situation involves a still more fundamental ambiguity. *One-Dimensional Man* will vacillate throughout between two contradictory hypotheses: (1) that advanced industrial society is capable of containing qualitative change for the foreseeable future; (2) that forces and tendencies exist which may break this containment and explode the society. I do not think that a clear answer can be given. Both tendencies are there, side by side—and even the one in the other. The first tendency is dominant, and whatever preconditions for a reversal may exist are being used to prevent it. Perhaps an accident may alter the situation, but unless the recognition of what is being done and what is being prevented subverts the consciousness and the behavior of man, not even a catastrophe will bring about the change.

The analysis is focused on advanced industrial society, in which the technical apparatus of production and distribution (with an increasing sector of automation) functions, not as the sum-total of mere instruments which can be isolated from their social and political effects, but rather as a system which determines *a priori* the product of the apparatus as well as the operations of servicing and extending it. In this society, the productive apparatus tends to become totalitarian to the extent to which it determines not only the socially needed occupations, skills, and attitudes, but also individual needs and aspirations. It thus obliterates the opposition between the private and public existence, between individual and social needs. Technology serves to institute new, more effective, and more pleasant forms of social control and social cohesion. The totalitarian tendency of these controls seems to assert itself in still another sense—by spreading to the less developed and even to the preindustrial areas of the world, and by creating similarities in the development of capitalism and communism.

In the face of the totalitarian features of this society, the traditional notion of the "neutrality" of technology can no longer be maintained. Technology as such cannot be isolated from the use to which it is put; the technological society is a system of domination which operates already in the concept and construction of techniques.

The way in which a society organizes the life of its members involves an initial *choice* between historical alternatives which are determined by the inherited level of the material and intellectual

culture. The choice itself results from the play of the dominant interests. It *anticipates* specific modes of transforming and utilizing man
and nature and rejects other modes. It is one "project" of realization
among others.* But once the project has become operative in the
basic institutions and relations, it tends to become exclusive and to
determine the development of the society as a whole. As a technological universe, advanced industrial society is a political universe,
the latest stage in the realization of a specific historical project—
namely, the experience, transformation, and organization of nature
as the mere stuff of domination.

As the project unfolds, it shapes the entire universe of discourse
and action, intellectual and material culture. In the medium of technology, culture, politics, and the economy merge into an omnipresent
system which swallows up or repulses all alternatives. The productivity and growth potential of this system stabilize the society and
contain technical progress within the framework of domination.
Technological rationality has become political rationality.

---

* The term "project" emphasizes the element of freedom and responsibility in historical determination: it links autonomy and contingency. In this sense, the term is used
in the work of Jean-Paul Sartre.

16. THE BLACK PANTHER PARTY

What We Want, What We Believe

(1966)

The **"Black Panther Party Platform"** outlined what cofounder Huey P. Newton called "the essential points for the survival of Black and oppressed people in the United States." **THE BLACK PANTHER PARTY FOR SELF-DEFENSE** was formed in October 1966 in Oakland, California, by Newton and Bobby Seale, and it soon became the most storied black militant organization of the late 1960s. The Panthers called for African Americans to arm themselves in self-defense, and in their early days they followed police cars that patrolled black neighborhoods to see that the police didn't violate anyone's civil rights. Accordingly, they were the target of severe harassment and infiltration from law enforcement agencies, and they were involved in several violent confrontations with police. During the early 1970s the group's influence waned under the pressures of government repression, legal difficulties, and internal schisms.

SOURCE: Reprinted in Deirdre Mullane, *Crossing the Danger Water: Three Hundred Years of African-American Writing.* New York: Doubleday, 1993.

SELECTED READINGS: Charles E. Jones, ed., *The Black Panther Party (Reconsidered)* (1998). Hugh Pearson, *The Shadow of the Panther: Huey Newton and the Price of Black Power in America* (1994). Huey P. Newton, *Revolutionary Suicide* (1973).

1. *We want freedom. We want power to determine the destiny of our Black Community.*

We believe that black people will not be free until we are able to determine our destiny.

2. *We want full employment for our people.*

We believe that the federal government is responsible and obligated to give every man employment or a guaranteed income. We believe that if the white American businessmen will not give full employment, then the means of production should be taken from the businessmen and placed in the community so that the people of the community can organize and employ all of its people and give a high standard of living.

3. *We want an end to the robbery by the white man of our Black Community.*

We believe that this racist government has robbed us and now we are demanding the overdue debt of forty acres and two mules. Forty acres and two mules was promised 100 years ago as restitution for [the] slave labor and mass murder of black people. We will accept the payment in currency which will be distributed to our many communities. The Germans are now aiding the Jews in Israel for the genocide of the Jewish people. The Germans murdered six million Jews. The American racist has taken part in the slaughter of over fifty million black people; therefore, we feel that this is a modest demand that we make.

4. *We want decent housing, fit for shelter of human beings.*

We believe that if the white landlords will not give decent housing to our black community, then the housing and the land should be made into cooperatives so that our community, with government aid, can build and make decent housing for its people.

5. *We want education for our people that exposes the true nature of this decadent American society. We want education that teaches us our true history and our role in the present-day society.*

We believe in an education system that will give to our people a knowledge of self. If a man does not have knowledge of himself and his position in society and the world, then he has little chance to relate to anything else.

6. *We want all black men to be exempt from military service.*

We believe that black people should not be forced to fight in the military service to defend a racist government that does not protect us. We will not fight and kill other people of color in the world who, like the black people, are being victimized by the white racist government of America. We will protect ourselves from the force and violence of the racist police and the racist military, by whatever means necessary.

7. *We want an immediate end to POLICE BRUTALITY and MURDER of black people.*

We believe we can end police brutality in our black community by organizing black self-defense groups that are dedicated to defending our black community from racist police oppression and brutality. The Second Amendment to the Constitution of the United States gives us a right to bear arms. We therefore believe that all black people should arm themselves for self-defense.

8. *We want freedom for all black men held in federal, state, county and city prisons and jails.*

We believe that all black people should be released from the many jails and prisons because they have not received a fair and impartial trial.

9. *We want all black people when brought to trial to be tried in court by a jury of their peer group or people from their black communities, as defined by the Constitution of the United States.*

We believe that the courts should follow the United States Constitution so that black people will receive fair trials. The 14th Amendment of the U.S. Constitution gives a man a right to be tried by his peer group. A peer is a person from a similar economic, social, religious, geographical, environmental, historical and racial background. To do this, the court will be forced to select a jury from the black community from which the black defendant came. We have been, and are being, tried by all-white juries that have no understanding of the "average reasoning man" of the black community.

10. *We want land, bread, housing, education, clothing, justice and peace. And as our major political objective, a United Nations—supervised plebiscite to be held throughout the black colony in which only black colonial subjects*

will be allowed to participate, for the purpose of determining the will of black people as to their national destiny.

When, in the course of human events, it becomes necessary for one people to dissolve the political bands which have connected them with another, and to assume, among the powers of the earth, the separate and equal station to which the laws of nature and nature's God entitle them, a decent respect to the opinions of mankind requires that they should declare the causes which impel them to the separation.

We hold these truths to be self-evident, that all men are created equal; that they are endowed by their Creator with certain unalienable rights; that among these are life, liberty, and the pursuit of happiness. *That, to secure these rights, governments are instituted among men, deriving their just powers from the consent of the governed; that, whenever any form of government becomes destructive of these ends, it is the right of the people to alter or to abolish it, and to institute a new government, laying its foundation on such principles, and organizing its powers in such form, as to them shall seem most likely to effect their safety and happiness.* Prudence, indeed, will dictate that governments long established should not be changed for light and transient causes; and accordingly, all experience hath shown, that mankind are more disposed to suffer, while evils are sufferable, than to right themselves by abolishing the forms to which they are accustomed. *But, when a long train of abuses and usurpations pursuing invariably the same object, evinces a design to reduce them under absolute despotism, it is their right, it is their duty, to throw off such government, and to provide new guards for their future security.*

17. ROBIN MORGAN

No More Miss America!
(1968)

September 7, 1968, brought "women's lib" to national attention as approximately one hundred radical feminists protested that year's Miss America pageant in Atlantic City, New Jersey. The protest was largely organized by feminist icon **ROBIN MORGAN** (1941–), who was the primary author of the document reprinted below, and New York Radical Women (NYRW), the first women's liberation group in New York City. Morgan was born in Florida and grew up in New York, and she has been active in the international feminist movement since the 1960s. In 1970 she edited the pioneering feminist anthology, *Sisterhood Is Powerful*. At the 1968 Miss America Pageant, demonstrators argued that beauty pageants were degrading to women. In addition to picketing, they engaged in creative guerrilla theater, throwing various "instruments of torture to women" into a trash can (these included high-heeled shoes, bras, and copies of *Playboy* magazine) and bestowing a Miss America crown upon a sheep in an effort to raise women's consciousness. Later that night, several women disrupted the nationally televised pageant, unfurling a banner and shouting feminist slogans.

SOURCE: Robin Morgan. *Sisterhood Is Powerful: An Anthology of Writings from the Women's Liberation Movement.* New York: Vintage Books, 1970.

SELECTED READINGS: Kathleen C. Berkeley, *The Women's Liberation Movement in America* (1999). Alice Echols, *Daring to Be Bad: Radical Feminism in America, 1967–1975* (1989). Robin Morgan, *Going Too Far: The Personal Chronicle of a Feminist* (1977).

The Ten Points We Protest:

1. *The Degrading Mindless-Boob-Girlie Symbol.* The Pageant contestants epitomize the roles we are all forced to play as women. The parade down the runway blares the metaphor of the 4-H Club county fair, where the nervous animals are judged for teeth, fleece, etc., and where the best "specimen" gets the blue ribbon. So are women in our society forced daily to compete for male approval, enslaved by ludicrous "beauty" standards we ourselves are conditioned to take seriously.

2. *Racism with Roses.* Since its inception in 1921, the Pageant has not had one Black finalist, and this has not been for a lack of test-case contestants. There has never been a Puerto Rican, Alaskan, Hawaiian, or Mexican-American winner. Nor has there ever been a *true* Miss America—an American Indian.

3. *Miss America as Military Death Mascot.* The highlight of her reign each year is a cheerleader-tour of American troops abroad—last year she went to Vietnam to pep-talk our husbands, fathers, sons and boyfriends into dying and killing with a better spirit. She personifies the "unstained patriotic American womanhood our boys are fighting for." The Living Bra and the Dead Soldier. We refuse to be used as Mascots for Murder.

4. *The Consumer Con-Game.* Miss America is a walking commercial for the Pageant's sponsors. Wind her up and she plugs your product on promotion tours and TV—all in an "honest, objective" endorsement. What a shill.

5. *Competition Rigged and Unrigged.* We deplore the encouragement of an American myth that oppresses men as well as women: the win-or-you're-worthless competive disease. The "beauty contest" creates only one winner to be "used" and forty-nine losers who are "useless."

6. *The Woman as Pop Culture Obsolescent Theme.* Spindle, mutilate, and then discard tomorrow. What is so ignored as last year's Miss America? This only reflects the gospel of our society, according to Saint Male: women must be young, juicy, malleable—hence age discrimination and the cult of youth. And we women are brainwashed into believing this ourselves!

7. *The Unbeatable Madonna-Whore Combination.* Miss America and Playboy's centerfold are sisters over the skin. To win approval, we must be both sexy and wholesome, delicate but able to cope, demure yet titillatingly bitchy. Deviation of any sort brings, we are told, disaster: "You won't get a man!!"

8. *The Irrelevant Crown on the Throne of Mediocrity.* Miss America represents what women are supposed to be: unoffensive, bland, apolitical. If you are tall, short, over or under what weight The Man prescribes you should be, forget it. Personality, articulateness, intelligence, commitment—unwise. Conformity is the key to the crown—and, by extension, to success in our society.

9. *Miss America as Dream Equivalent To*—? In this reputedly democratic society, where every little boy supposedly can grow up to be President, what can every little girl hope to grow to be? Miss America. That's where it's at. Real power to control our own lives is restricted to men, while women get patronizing pseudo-power, an ermine cloak and a bunch of flowers; men are judged by their actions, women by their appearance.

10. *Miss America as Big Sister Watching You.* The Pageant exercises Thought Control, attempts to sear the Image onto our minds, to further make women oppressed and men oppressors; to enslave us all the more in high-heeled, low-status roles; to inculcate false values in young girls; to use women as beasts of buying; to seduce us to prostitute ourselves before our own oppression.

NO MORE MISS AMERICA

18. ABBIE HOFFMAN

Chicago 8 Trial Testimony
(1968)

ABBOT HOWARD ("ABBIE") HOFFMAN (1936–1989) was a leading counter-cultural activist of the late 1960s. He was born in Worcester, Massachusetts, and he was educated at Brandeis University and the University of California at Berkeley, where he earned an M.A. in psychology. Along with several others, Hoffman helped to pioneer a humorous and theatrical style of protest that helped to draw many people into the Movement. One of his famous stunts was to throw money off the balcony of the New York Stock Exchange, thereby creating a small frenzy and demonstrating, he said, the greed of those who worked on Wall Street. In 1967, he helped organize a sit-in at the Pentagon by promising to help "levitate" the building in order to rid it of its evil spirits. In 1968, he helped organize the farcical Youth International Party ("Yippies") which protested at that year's Democratic National Convention. While there, he was arrested, and later he was put on trial, along with seven others, for conspiracy to travel interstate "with the intent to . . . riot." His legal strategy, on display below, was to openly mock the proceedings and to try to build support for the burgeoning youth culture. The judge, Julius Hoffman (obviously no relation), became notorious for being so incredibly biased in favor of the prosecution. With four others, Hoffman was found guilty and sentenced to prison, but his conviction was later overturned. In 1973, Hoffman was caught trying to buy cocaine in a sting operation. He skipped bail, and lived underground until 1980, when he turned himself in to authorities and spent about a year in jail. Hoffman suffered from bi-polar disorder, and he committed suicide in 1989.

SOURCE: http://www.law.umkc.edu/faculty/projects/FTrials/Chicago7/Hoffman.html

SELECTED READINGS: Abbie Hoffman, *The Best of Abbie Hoffman* (1989). Jonah Raskin, *For the Hell of It: The Life and Times of Abbie Hoffman* (1997). Jon Wiener, ed., *Conspiracy in the Streets: The Extraordinary Trial of the Chicago Eight* (2006).

MR. WEINGLASS: Will you please identify yourself for the record?

THE WITNESS: My name is Abbie. I am an orphan of America.

MR. SCHULTZ: Your Honor, may the record show it is the defendant Hoffman who has taken the stand?

THE COURT: Oh, yes. It may so indicate. . . .

MR. WEINGLASS: Where do you reside?

THE WITNESS: I live in Woodstock Nation.

MR. WEINGLASS: Will you tell the Court and jury where it is?

THE WITNESS: Yes. It is a nation of alienated young people. We carry it around with us as a state of mind in the same way as the Sioux Indians carried the Sioux nation around with them. It is a nation dedicated to cooperation versus competition, to the idea that people should have better means of exchange than property or money, that there should be some other basis for human interaction. It is a nation dedicated to—

THE COURT: Just where it is, that is all.

THE WITNESS: It is in my mind and in the minds of my brothers and sisters. It does not consist of property or material but, rather, of ideas and certain values. We believe in a society—

THE COURT: No, we want the place of residence, if he has one, place of doing business, if you have a business. Nothing about philosophy or India, sir. Just where you live, if you have a place to live. Now you said Woodstock. In what state is Woodstock?

THE WITNESS: It is in the state of mind, in the mind of myself and my brothers and sisters. It is a conspiracy. Presently, the nation is held captive, in the penitentiaries of the institutions of a decaying system.

MR. WEINGLASS: Can you tell the Court and jury your present age?

THE WITNESS: My age is 33. I am a child of the 60s.

MR. WEINGLASS: When were you born?

THE WITNESS: Psychologically, 1960.

MR. SCHULTZ: Objection, if the Court please. I move to strike the answer.

MR. WEINGLASS: What is the actual date of your birth?

THE WITNESS: November 30, 1936.

MR. WEINGLASS: Between the date of your birth, November 30, 1936, and May 1, 1960, what if anything occurred in your life?

THE WITNESS: Nothing. I believe it is called an American education.

MR. SCHULTZ: Objection.

THE COURT: I sustain the objection.

THE WITNESS: Huh.

MR. WEINGLASS: Abbie, could you tell the Court and jury—

MR. SCHULTZ: His name isn't Abbie. I object to this informality.

MR. WEINGLASS: Can you tell the Court and jury what is your present occupation?

THE WITNESS: I am a cultural revolutionary. Well, I am really a defendant—full-time.

MR. WEINGLASS: What do you mean by the phrase "cultural revolutionary?"

THE WITNESS: Well, I suppose it is a person who tries to shape and participate in the values, and the mores, the customs and the style of living of new people who eventually become inhabitants of a new nation and a new society through art and poetry, theater, and music.

MR. WEINGLASS: What have you done yourself to participate in that revolution?

THE WITNESS: Well, I have been a rock and roll singer. I am a reporter with the Liberation News Service. I am a poet. I am a film maker. I made a movie called "Yippies Tour Chicago or How I Spent My

Summer Vacation." Currently, I am negotiating with United Artists and MGM to do a movie in Hollywood.

I have written an extensive pamphlet on how to live free in the city of New York.

I have written two books, one called *Revolution for the Hell of It* under the pseudonym Free, and one called *Woodstock Nation*.

MR. WEINGLASS: Taking you back to the spring of 1960, approximately May 1, 1960, will you tell the Court and jury where you were?

MR. SCHULTZ: 1960?

THE WITNESS: That's right.

MR. SCHULTZ: Objection.

THE COURT: I sustain the objection.

MR. WEINGLASS: Your Honor, that date has great relevance to the trial. May 1, 1960, was this witness's first public demonstration. I am going to bring him down through Chicago.

THE COURT: Not in my presence, you are not going to bring him down. I sustain the objection to the question.

THE WITNESS: My background has nothing to do with my state of mind?

THE COURT: Will you remain quiet while I am making a ruling? I know you have no respect for me.

MR. KUNSTLER: Your Honor, that is totally unwarranted. I think your remarks call for a motion for a mistrial.

THE COURT: And your motion calls for a denial of the motion. Mr. Weinglass, continue with your examination.

MR. KUNSTLER: You denied my motion? I hadn't even started to argue it.

THE COURT: I don't need any argument on that one. The witness turned his back on me while he was on the witness stand.

THE WITNESS: I was just looking at the pictures of the long hairs up on the wall. . . .

THE COURT: . . . I will let the witness tell about this asserted conversation with Mr. Rubin on the occasion described.

MR. WEINGLASS: What was the conversation at that time?

THE WITNESS: Jerry Rubin told me that he had come to New York to be project director of a peace march in Washington that was going to march to the Pentagon in October, October 21. He said that the peace movement suffered from a certain kind of attitude, mainly that it was based solely on the issue of the Vietnam war. He said that the war in Vietnam was not just an accident but a direct by-product of the kind of system, a capitalist system in the country, and that we had to begin to put forth new kinds of values, especially to young people in the country, to make a kind of society in which a Vietnam war would not be possible.

And he felt that these attitudes and values were present in the hippie movement and many of the techniques, the guerrilla theater techniques, that had been used and many of these methods of communication would allow for people to participate and become involved in a new kind of democracy.

I said that the Pentagon was a five-sided evil symbol in most religions and that it might be possible to approach this from a religious point of view. If we got large numbers of people to surround the Pentagon, we could exorcize it of its evil spirits.

So I had agreed at that point to begin working on the exorcism of the Pentagon demonstration.

MR. WEINGLASS: Prior to the date of the demonstration, which is October, did you go to the Pentagon?

THE WITNESS: Yes. I went about a week or two before with one of my close brothers, Martin Carey, a poster maker, and we measured the Pentagon, the two of us, to see how many people would fit around it. We only had to do one side because it is just multiplied by five.

We got arrested. It's illegal to measure the Pentagon. I didn't know it up to that point.

When we were arrested they asked us what we were doing. We said it was to measure the Pentagon and we wanted a permit to raise it 300 feet in the air, and they said "How about 10?" So we said "OK."

And they threw us out of the Pentagon and we went back to New York and had a press conference, told them what it was about.

We also introduced a drug called *lace*, which, when you squirted it at the policemen made them take their clothes off and make love, a very potent drug.

MR. WEINGLASS: Did you mean literally that the building was to rise up 300 feet off the ground?

MR. SCHULTZ: I can't cross-examine about his meaning literally.

THE COURT: I sustain the objection.

MR. SCHULTZ: I would ask Mr. Weinglass please get on with the trial of this case and stop playing around with raising the Pentagon 10 feet or 300 feet off the ground.

MR. WEINGLASS: Your Honor, I am glad to see Mr. Schultz finally concedes that things like levitating the Pentagon building, putting LSD in the water, 10,000 people walking nude on Lake Michigan, and a $200,000 bribe attempt are all playing around. I am willing to concede that fact that it was all playing around, it was a play idea of this witness, and if he is willing to concede it, we can all go home.

THE COURT: I sustain the objection.

MR. WEINGLASS: Did you intend that the people who surrounded the Pentagon should do anything of a violent nature whatever to cause the building to rise 300 feet in the air and be exorcised of evil spirits?

MR. SCHULTZ: Objection.

THE COURT: I sustain the objection.

MR. WEINGLASS: Could you indicate to the Court and jury whether or not the Pentagon was, in fact, exorcised of its evil spirits?

THE WITNESS: Yes, I believe it was. . . .

MR. WEINGLASS: Now, drawing your attention to the first week of December 1967, did you have occasion to meet with Jerry Rubin and the others?

THE WITNESS: Yes.

MR. WEINGLASS: Will you relate to the Court and jury what the conversation was?

THE WITNESS: Yes.

We talked about the possibility of having demonstrations at the Democratic Convention in Chicago, Illinois, that was going to be occurring that August. I am not sure that we knew at that point that it was in Chicago. Wherever it was, we were planning on going.

Jerry Rubin, I believe, said that it would be a good idea to call it the Festival of Life in contrast to the Convention of Death, and to have it in some kind of public area, like a park or something, in Chicago.

One thing that I was very particular about was that we didn't have any concept of leadership involved. There was a feeling of young people that they didn't want to listen to leaders. We had to create a kind of situation in which people would be allowed to participate and become in a real sense their own leaders.

I think it was then after this that Paul Krassner said the word "YIPPIE," and we felt that that expressed in a kind of slogan and advertising sense the spirit that we wanted to put forth in Chicago, and we adopted that as our password, really. . . .

Anita [Hoffman] said that "Yippie" would be understood by our generation, that straight newspapers like the *New York Times* and the U.S. Government and the courts and everything wouldn't take it seriously unless it had a formal name, so she came up with the name: "Youth International Party." She said we could play a lot of jokes on the concept of "party" because everybody would think that we were this huge international conspiracy, but that in actuality we were a party that you had fun at.

Nancy [Kursham] said that fun was an integral ingredient, that people in America, because they were being programmed like IBM cards, weren't having enough fun in life and that if you watched television, the only people that you saw having any fun were people who were buying lousy junk on television commercials, and that this would be a whole new attitude because you would see people, young people, having fun while they were protesting the system, and that young people all around this country and around the world would be turned on for that kind of an attitude.

I said that fun was very important, too, that it was a direct rebuttal of the kind of ethics and morals that were being put forth in the country to keep people working in a rat race which didn't make any sense because in a few years that machines would do all the work anyway, that there was a whole system of values that people were taught to postpone their pleasure, to put all their money in the bank, to buy life insurance, a whole bunch of things that didn't make any sense to our generation at all, and that fun actually was becoming quite subversive.

Jerry said that because of our action at the Stock Exchange in throwing out the money, that within a few weeks the Wall Street brokers there had totally enclosed the whole stock exchange in bulletproof, shatterproof glass that cost something like $20,000 because they were afraid we'd come back and throw money out again.

He said that for hundreds of years political cartoonists had always pictured corrupt politicians in the guise of a pig, and he said that it would be great theater if we ran a pig for President, and we all took that on as like a great idea and that's more or less—that was the founding.

MR. WEINGLASS: The document that is before you, D-222 for identification, what is that document?

THE WITNESS: It was our initial call to people to describe what Yippie was about and why we were coming to Chicago.

MR. WEINGLASS: Now, Abbie, could you read the entire document to the jury.

THE WITNESS: It says:

"A STATEMENT FROM YIP!

"Join us in Chicago in August for an international festival of youth, music, and theater. Rise up and abandon the creeping meatball! Come all you rebels, youth spirits, rock minstrels, truth-seekers, peacock-freaks, poets, barricade-jumpers, dancers, lovers and artists!

"It is summer. It is the last week in August, and the NATIONAL DEATH PARTY meets to bless Lyndon Johnson. We are there! There are 50,000 of us dancing in the streets, throbbing with amplifiers and harmony. We are making love in the parks. We are reading, singing, laughing, printing newspapers, groping, and making a mock convention, and celebrating the birth of FREE AMERICA in our own time.

"Everything will be free. Bring blankets, tents, draft-cards, body-paint, Mr. Leary's Cow, food to share, music, eager skin, and happiness. The threats of LBJ, Mayor Daley, and J. Edgar Freako will not stop us. We are coming! We are coming from all over the world!

"The life of the American spirit is being torn asunder by the forces of violence, decay, and the napalm-cancer fiend. We demand the Politics of Ecstasy! We are the delicate spores of the new fierceness that will change America. We will create our own reality, we are Free America! And we will not accept the false theater of the Death Convention.

"We will be in Chicago. Begin preparations now! Chicago is yours! Do it!"

"Do it!" was a slogan like "Yippie." We use that a lot and it meant that each person that came should take on the responsibility for being his own leader—that we should, in fact, have a leaderless society.

We shortly thereafter opened an office and people worked in the office on what we call movement salaries, subsistence, thirty dollars a week. We had what the straight world would call a staff and an office, although we called it an energy center and regarded ourselves as a tribe or a family.

MR. WEINGLASS: Could you explain to the Court and jury, if you know, how this staff functioned in your office?

THE WITNESS: Well, I would describe it as anarchistic. People would pick up the phone and give information and people from all over the country were now becoming interested and they would ask for more information, whether we were going to get a permit, how the people in Chicago were relating, and would we bring flyers and banners and posters. We would have large general meetings that were open to anybody who wanted to come.

MR. WEINGLASS: How many people would attend these weekly meetings?

THE WITNESS: There were about two- to three hundred people there that were attending the meetings. Eventually we had to move into Union Square and hold meetings out in the public. There would be maybe three- to five hundred people attending meetings. . . .

MR. WEINGLASS: Where did you go [March 23], if you can recall?

THE WITNESS: I flew to Chicago to observe a meeting being sponsored, I believe, by the National Mobilization Committee. It was held at a place called Lake Villa, I believe, about twenty miles outside of Chicago here.

MR. WEINGLASS: Do you recall how you were dressed for that meeting?

THE WITNESS: I was dressed as an Indian. I had gone to Grand Central Station as an Indian, and so I just got on a plane and flew as an Indian.

MR. WEINGLASS: Now, when you flew to Chicago, were you alone?

THE WITNESS: No. Present were Jerry, myself, Paul Krassner, and Marshall Bloom, the head of this Liberation News Service.

MR. WEINGLASS: When you arrived at Lake Villa, did you have occasion to meet any of the defendants who are seated here at this table?

THE WITNESS: Yes, I met for the first time Rennie, Tom Hayden—who I had met before, and that's it, you know. . . .

MR. WEINGLASS: Was any decision reached at that meeting about coming to Chicago?

THE WITNESS: I believe that they debated for two days about whether they should come or not to Chicago. They decided to have more meetings. We said we had already made up our minds to come to Chicago and we passed out buttons and posters and said that if they were there, good, it would be a good time.

MR. WEINGLASS: Following the Lake Villa conference, do you recall where you went?

THE WITNESS: Yes. The next day, March 25, 1 went to the Aragon Ballroom. It was a benefit to raise money again for the Yippies but we had a meeting backstage in one of the dressing rooms with the Chicago Yippies.

MR. WEINGLASS: Do you recall what was discussed?

THE WITNESS: Yes. We drafted a permit application for the Festival to take place in Chicago. We agreed that Grant Park would be best.

MR. WEINGLASS: Directing your attention to the following morning, which was Monday morning, March 26, do you recall where you were at that morning?

THE WITNESS: We went to the Parks Department. Jerry was there, Paul, Helen Runningwater, Abe Peck, Reverend John Tuttle—there were a group of about twenty to thirty people, Yippies.

MR. WEINGLASS: Did you meet with anyone at the Park District at that time?

THE WITNESS: Yes. There were officials from the Parks Department to greet us, they took us into this office, and we presented a permit application.

MR. WEINGLASS: Did you ever receive a reply to this application?

THE WITNESS: Not to my knowledge.

MR. WEINGLASS: After your meeting with the Park District, where, if anywhere, did you go?

THE WITNESS: We held a brief press conference on the lawn in front of the Parks Department, and then we went to see Mayor Daley at City Hall. When we arrived, we were told that the mayor was indisposed and that Deputy Mayor David Stahl would see us.

MR. WEINGLASS: When you met with Deputy Mayor Stahl, what, if anything, occurred?

THE WITNESS: Helen Runningwater presented him with a copy of the permit application that we had submitted to the Parks Department. It was rolled up in the Playmate of the Month [and] said "To Dick with Love, the Yippies," on it. And we presented it to him and gave him a kiss and put a Yippie button on him, and when he opened it up, the Playmate was just there.

And he was very embarrassed by the whole thing, and he said that we had followed the right procedure, the city would give it proper attention and things like that. . . .

19. STUDENTS FOR A DEMOCRATIC SOCIETY

Bring the War Home
(1969)

Faced with the intransigence of the Vietnam War and the persistence of racism and police repression against the Black Panthers and other militants, in 1969 an ultraradical faction of **STUDENTS FOR A DEMOCRATIC SOCIETY (SDS)** named Weatherman began calling for armed revolutionary struggle against the United States. (The group got its name from the Bob Dylan lyric, "You don't need a weatherman to know which way the wind blows.") Although they represented only a tiny minority of SDS's actual membership, they drew an enormous amount of media attention and bombed many symbolic targets. "Bring the War Home," was a popular Weatherman brochure (written under the auspices of SDS) that called for a "National Action" in Chicago in 1969, in response to the police riot at the 1968 Democratic National Convention. This protest, also dubbed the "Days of Rage," attracted only a few hundred demonstrators and involved property damage and violent confrontation with the police.

SOURCE: *New Left Notes.* August 1, 1969.

SELECTED READINGS: Jeremy Varon, *Utopia, Revolution, and Violence: The Weather Underground and the Red Army Faction* (2003). Bill Ayers, *Fugitive Days: A Memoir* (2001). Kirkpatrick Sale, *SDS* (1973).

Look at It: America, 1969

The war goes on, despite the jive double-talk about troop withdrawals and peace talks. Black people continue to be murdered by agents of the fat cats who run this country, if not in one way, then in another: by the pigs or the courts, by the boss or the welfare department.

Working people face higher taxes, inflation, speed-ups, and the sure knowledge—if it hasn't happened already—that their sons may be shipped off to Vietnam and shipped home in a box. And young people all over the country go to prisons that are called schools, are trained for jobs that don't exist or serve no one's real interest but the boss's, and, to top it all off, get told that Vietnam is the place to defend their "freedom."

None of this is very new. The cities have been falling apart, the schools have been bullshit, the jobs have been rotten and unfulfilling for a long time.

What's new is that today not quite so many people are confused, and a lot more people are angry: angry about the fact that the promises we have heard since first grade are all jive; angry that, when you get down to it, this system is nothing but the total economic and military put-down of the oppressed peoples of the world.

And more: it's a system that steals the goods, the resources, and the labor of poor and working people all over the world in order to fill the pockets and bank accounts of a tiny capitalist class. (Call it imperialism.) It's a system that divides white workers from blacks by offering whites crumbs off the table, and telling them that if they don't stay cool the blacks will move in on their jobs, their homes, and their schools. (Call it white supremacy.) It's a system that divides men from women, forcing women to be subservient to men from childhood, to be slave labor in the home and cheap labor in the factory. (Call it male supremacy.) And it's a system that has colonized whole nations within this country—the nation of black people, the nation of brown people—to enslave, oppress, and ultimately murder the people on whose backs this country was built. (Call it fascism.)

But the lies are catching up to America—and the slick rich people and their agents in the government bureaucracies, the courts, the schools, and the pig stations just can't cut it anymore.

Black and brown people know it.

Young people know it.

More and more white working people know it.

And you know it.

SDS Is Calling the Action This Year

But it will be a different action. An action not only against a single war or a "foreign policy," but against the whole imperialist system that made that war a necessity. An action not only for immediate withdrawal of all U.S. occupation troops, but in support of the heroic fight of the Vietnamese people and the National Liberation Front for freedom and independence. An action not only to bring "peace to Vietnam," but beginning to establish another front against imperialism right here in America—to "bring the war home."

We are demanding that all occupational troops get out of Vietnam and every other place they don't belong. This includes the black and brown communities, the workers' picket lines, the high schools, and the streets of Berkeley. No longer will we tolerate "law and order" backed up by soldiers in Vietnam and pigs in the communities and schools; a "law and order" that serves only the interests of those in power and tries to smash the people down whenever they rise up.

We are demanding the release of all political prisoners who have been victimized by the ever-growing attacks on the black liberation struggle and the people in general. Especially the leaders of the black liberation struggle like Huey P. Newton, Ahmed Evans, Fred Hampton, and Martin Sostre.

We are expressing total support for the National Liberation Front and the newly formed Provisional Revolutionary Government of South Vietnam. Throughout the history of the war, the NLF has provided political and military leadership to the people of South Vietnam. The Provisional Revolutionary Government, recently formed by the NLF and other groups, has pledged to "mobilize the South Vietnamese armed forces and people" in order to continue the struggle for independence. The PRG also has expressed solidarity with "the just struggle of the Afro-American people for their fundamental national rights," and has pledged to "actively support the national independence movements of Asia, Africa, and Latin America."

We are also expressing total support for the black liberation struggle, part of the same struggle that the Vietnamese are fighting, against the same enemy.

We are demanding independence for Puerto Rico, and an end to the colonial oppression that the Puerto Rican nation faces at the hands of U.S. imperialism.

We are demanding an end to the surtax, a tax taken from the working people of this country and used to kill working people in Vietnam and other places for fun and profit.

We are expressing solidarity with the Conspiracy 8 who led the struggle last summer in Chicago. Our action is planned to roughly coincide with the beginning of their trial.

And we are expressing support for GIs in Vietnam and throughout the world who are being made to fight the battles of the rich, like poor and working people have always been made to do. We support those GIs at Fort Hood, Fort Jackson, and many other army bases who have refused to be cannon fodder in a war against the people of Vietnam.

It's Almost Hard to Remember When the War Began

But, after years of peace marches, petitions, and the gradual realization that this war was no "mistake" at all, one critical fact remains: the war is not just happening in Vietnam.

It is happening in the jungles of Guatemala, Bolivia, Thailand, and all oppressed nations throughout the world.

And it is happening here. In black communities throughout the country. On college campuses. And in the high schools, in the shops, and on the streets.

It is a war in which there are only two sides; a war not for domination but for an end to domination, not for destruction, but for liberation and the unchaining of human freedom.

And it is a war in which we cannot "resist"; it is a war in which we must fight.

On October 11, tens of thousands of people will come to Chicago to bring the war home. Join us.

20. CÉSAR CHÁVEZ

Letter From Delano

(1969)

In his famous "Letter From Delano," **CÉSAR CHÁVEZ** explained the United Farm Workers' (UFW) grievances against the "agribusiness" system that kept workers in poverty and forced them to toil amidst toxic poisons in vineyards. Chávez (1927–1993) was born near Yuma, Arizona, and was a migrant worker for many years before he became a full-time organizer. He served as general director of the Community Service Organization (CSO) in California from 1958 to 1962, and in 1966 he helped create the UFW. With a variety of nonviolent tactics, including strikes, fasts, picketing, and marches, Chávez won many labor victories, including an important one against American table-grape growers in 1970. Modeled in part upon Martin Luther King, Jr.'s, "Letter From A Birmingham Jail," Chávez's "Letter from Delano" was originally published in *Christian Century* magazine, and it drew national attention to the dreadful working conditions on many American farms.

SOURCE: César Chávez. "Letter from Delano." *Christian Century.* April 23, 1969.

SELECTED READINGS: Susan Ferriss, *The Fight in the Fields: César Chávez and the Farmworkers Movement* (1997). Richard Griswold del Castillo, *César Chávez: A Triumph of Spirit* (1995). John Gregory Dunne, *Delano:*

The Story of the California Grape Strike (1967). Marshall Ganz, *Why David Sometimes Wins: Leadership, Organization, and Strategy in the California Farm Worker Movement* (2009).

"We are not Beasts of Burden . . . we are Men"

Dear Mr. Barr [President, California Grape and Tree Fruit League]:

I am sad to hear about your accusations in the press that our union movement and table grape boycott have been successful because we have used violence and terror tactics. If what you say is true, I have been a failure and should withdraw from the struggle; but you are left with the awesome moral responsibility, before God and man, to come forward with whatever information you have so that corrective action can begin at once. If for any reason you fail to come forth to substantiate your charges, then you must be held responsible for committing violence against us, albeit violence of the tongue. I am convinced that you as a human being did not mean what you said but rather acted hastily under pressure from the public relations firm that has been hired to try to counteract the tremendous moral force of our movement. How many times we ourselves have felt the need to lash out in anger and bitterness.

Today on Good Friday 1969 we remember the life and the sacrifice of Martin Luther King, Jr., who gave himself totally to the nonviolent struggle for peace and justice. In his "Letter from Birmingham Jail" Dr. King describes better than I could our hopes for the strike and boycott: "Injustice must be exposed, with all the tension its exposure creates, to the light of human conscience and the air of national opinion before it can be cured." For our part I admit that we have seized upon every tactic and strategy consistent with the morality of our cause to expose that injustice and thus to heighten the sensitivity of the American conscience so that farm workers will have without bloodshed their own union and the dignity of bargaining with their agribusiness employers. By lying about the nature of our movement, Mr. Barr, you are working against nonviolent social change. Unwittingly perhaps, you may unleash that other force which our union by discipline and deed, censure and education, has sought to avoid, that panacean shortcut: that sense-less violence which honors no color, class or neighborhood.

You must understand—I must make you understand—that our membership and the hopes and aspirations of the hundreds of thou-sands of the poor and dispossessed that have been raised on our account are, above all, human beings, no better and no worse than any other cross-section of human society; we are not saints because we are poor, but by the same measure neither are we immoral. We are men and women who have suffered and endured much, and not only because of our object poverty but because we have been kept poor. The colors of our skins, the languages of our cultural and native origins, the lack of formal education, the exclusion from the democratic process, the numbers of our slain in recent wars—all these burdens generation after generation have sought to demoralize us, to break our human spirit. But God knows that we are not beasts of burden, agricultural implements or rented slaves; we are men. And mark this well, Mr. Barr, we are men locked in a death struggle against man's inhumanity to man in the industry that you represent. And this struggle itself gives meaning to our life and ennobles our dying.

As your industry has experienced, our strikers here in Delano and those who represent us throughout the world are well trained for this struggle. They have been under the gun, they have been kicked and beaten and herded by dogs, they have been cursed and ridiculed, they have been stripped and chained and jailed, they have been sprayed with the poisons used in the vineyards; but they have been taught not to lie down and die nor to flee in shame, but to resist with every ounce of human endurance and spirit. To resist not with retaliation in kind but to overcome with love and compassion, with ingenuity and creativity, with hard work and longer hours, with stamina and patient tenacity, with truth and public appeal, with friends and allies, with mobility and discipline, with politics and law, and with prayer and fasting. They were not trained in a month or even a year; after all, this new harvest season will mark our fourth full year of strike and even now we continue to plan and prepare for the years to come. Time accomplishes for the poor what money does for the rich.

This is not to pretend that we have everywhere been successful enough or that we have not made mistakes. And while we do not belittle or underestimate our adversaries—for they are the rich and the powerful and they possess the land—we are not afraid nor do we cringe from the confrontation. We welcome it! We have planned for it. We know that our cause is just, that history is a story of social revolution, and that the poor shall inherit the land.

Once again, I appeal to you as the representative of your industry and as a man. I ask you to recognize and bargain with our union before the economic pressure of the boycott and strike takes an irrevocable toll; but if not, I ask you to at least sit down with us to discuss the safeguards necessary to keep our historical struggle free of violence. I make this appeal because as one of the leaders of our nonviolent movement, I know and accept my responsibility for preventing, if possible, the destruction of human life and property. For these reasons, and knowing of Gandhi's admonition that fasting is the last resort in place of the sword, during a most critical time in our movement last February 1968 I undertook a 25-day fast. I repeat to you the principle enunciated to the membership at the start of the fast: if to build our union required the deliberate taking of life, either the life of a grower or his child, or the life of a farm worker or his child, then I choose not to see the union built.

Mr. Barr, let me be painfully honest with you. You must understand these things. We advocate militant nonviolence as our means for social revolution and to achieve justice for our people, but we are not blind or deaf to the desperate and moody winds of human frustration, impatience and rage that blow among us. Gandhi himself admitted that if his only choice were cowardice or violence, he would choose violence. Men are not angels, and time and tide wait for no man. Precisely because of these powerful human emotions, we have tried to involve masses of people in their own struggle. Participation and self-determination remain the best experience of freedom, and free men instinctively prefer democratic change and even protect the rights guaranteed to seek it. Only the enslaved in despair have need of violent overthrow.

This letter does not express all that is in my heart, Mr. Barr. But if it says nothing else, it says that we do not hate you or rejoice to see your industry destroyed; we hate the agribusiness system that seeks to keep us enslaved, and we shall overcome and change it not by retaliation or bloodshed but by a determined nonviolent struggle carried on by those masses of farm workers who intend to be free and human.

21. NOAM CHOMSKY

The Responsibility of Intellectuals
(1969)

NOAM CHOMSKY (1928–) is a pioneering linguist and perhaps the world's most prolific radical critic of American imperialism. He was born in Philadelphia and he earned his B.A., M.A., and Ph.D. from the University of Pennsylvania, finishing the latter degree in 1955. That year, he joined the faculty at the Massachusetts Institute of Technology (MIT) and was made full professor in 1961. When his essay "The Responsibility of Intellectuals" appeared in the *New York Review of Books* in 1967, Chomsky emerged as a leading critic of the Vietnam War. In addition to attacking American foreign policy (which he observes has frequently involved the undermining of democratically elected governments and the propping up of corrupt dictators), Chomsky has scornfully documented the Establishmentarian mindset of the media, the failures and the hypocrisies of the so-called "war on drugs," and the inequalities promoted by capitalism. Chomsky has written scores of books in both linguistics and politics, and he has won a broad following in the United States and across the world, despite the fact that the American mainstream media has largely ignored his work. In 2006, however, Venezuela president Hugo Chávez recommended Chomsky's *Hegemony or Survival* while addressing the United Nations, prompting a tremendous spike in sales. In addition to his written work, Chomsky continues to lecture widely.

SOURCE: Noam Chomsky, "A Special Supplement: The Responsibility of Intellectuals," *The New York Review of Books*, February 23, 1967.

SELECTED READINGS: Robert F. Barksy, *The Chomsky Effect: A Radical Works Beyond the Ivory Tower* (2007). Noam Chomsky, *The Chomsky Reader*, ed. James Peck (1987). Noam Chomsky, *Hegemony or Survival: America's Quest for Global Dominance* (2003).

. . . IT IS THE RESPONSIBILITY of intellectuals to speak the truth and to expose lies. This, at least, may seem enough of a truism to pass over without comment. Not so, however. For the modern intellectual, it is not at all obvious. Thus we have Martin Heidegger writing, in a pro-Hitler declaration of 1933, that "truth is the revelation of that which makes a people certain, clear, and strong in its action and knowledge"; it is only this kind of "truth" that one has a responsibility to speak. Americans tend to be more forthright. When Arthur Schlesinger was asked by *The New York Times* in November, 1965, to explain the contradiction between his published account of the Bay of Pigs incident and the story he had given the press at the time of the attack, he simply remarked that he had lied; and a few days later, he went on to compliment the *Times* for also having suppressed information on the planned invasion, in "the national interest," as this term was defined by the group of arrogant and deluded men of whom Schlesinger gives such a flattering portrait in his recent account of the Kennedy Administration. It is of no particular interest that one man is quite happy to lie in behalf of a cause which he knows to be unjust; but it is significant that such events provoke so little response in the intellectual community—for example, no one has said that there is something strange in the offer of a major chair in the humanities to a historian who feels it to be his duty to persuade the world that an American-sponsored invasion of a nearby country is nothing of the sort. And what of the incredible sequence of lies on the part of our government and its spokesmen concerning such matters as negotiations in Vietnam? The facts are known to all who care to know. The press, foreign and domestic, has presented documentation to refute each falsehood as it appears. But the power of the government's propaganda apparatus is such that the citizen who does not undertake a research project on the subject can hardly hope to confront government pronouncements with fact.

The deceit and distortion surrounding the American invasion of Vietnam is by now so familiar that it has lost its power to shock. It is therefore useful to recall that although new levels of cynicism are constantly being reached, their clear antecedents were accepted at home with quiet toleration. It is a useful exercise to compare government statements at the time of the invasion of Guatemala in 1954 with Eisenhower's admission—to be more accurate, his boast—a decade later that American planes were sent "to help the invaders" (*New York Times*, October 14, 1965). Nor is it only in moments of crisis that duplicity is considered perfectly in order. "New Frontiersmen," for example, have scarcely distinguished themselves by a passionate concern for historical accuracy, even when they are not being called upon to provide a "propaganda cover" for ongoing actions. For example, Arthur Schlesinger (*New York Times*, February 6, 1966) describes the bombing of North Vietnam and the massive escalation of military commitment in early 1965 as based on a "perfectly rational argument":

> so long as the Vietcong thought they were going to win the war, they obviously would not be interested in any kind of negotiated settlement.

The date is important. Had this statement been made six months earlier, one could attribute it to ignorance. But this statement appeared after the UN, North Vietnamese, and Soviet initiatives had been front-page news for months. It was already public knowledge that these initiatives had preceeded the escalation of February 1965 and, in fact, continued for several weeks after the bombing began. Correspondents in Washington tried desperately to find some explanation for the startling deception that had been revealed. Chalmers Roberts, for example, wrote in the *Boston Globe* on November 19 with unconscious irony:

> [late February, 1965] hardly seemed to Washington to be a propitious moment for negotiations [since] Mr. Johnson . . . had just ordered the

first bombing of North Vietnam in an effort to bring Hanoi to a conference table where the bargaining chips on both sides would be more
closely matched.

Coming at that moment, Schlesinger's statement is less an example
of deceit than of contempt—contempt for an audience that can be
expected to tolerate such behavior with silence, if not approval. . . .

[Also] consider the remarks of Henry Kissinger in his concluding
remarks at the Harvard-Oxford television debate on America's Vietnam policies. He observed, rather sadly, that what disturbs him most
is that others question not our judgment, but our motives—a re-
markable comment by a man whose professional concern is political
analysis, that is, analysis of the actions of governments in terms of
motives that are unexpressed in official propaganda and perhaps
only dimly perceived by those whose acts they govern. No one would
be disturbed by an analysis of the political behavior of the Russians,
French, or Tanzanians questioning their motives and interpreting
their actions by the long-range interests concealed behind their official rhetoric. But it is an article of faith that American motives are pure,
and not subject to analysis. Although it is nothing new in American
intellectual history—or, for that matter, in the general history of imperialist apologia—this innocence becomes increasingly distasteful as
the power it serves grows more dominant in world affairs, and more
capable, therefore, of the unconstrained viciousness that the mass
media present to us each day. We are hardly the first power in history
to combine material interests, great technological capacity, and an
utter disregard for the suffering and misery of the lower orders. The
long tradition of naiveté and self-righteousness that disfigures our
intellectual history, however, must serve as a warning to the third
world, if such a warning is needed, as to how our protestations of
sincerity and benign intent are to be interpreted.

The basic assumptions of the "New Frontiersmen" should be pon-
dered carefully by those who look forward to the involvement of academic intellectuals in politics. For example, I have referred above to
Arthur Schlesinger's objections to the Bay of Pigs invasion, but the

reference was imprecise. True, he felt that it was a "terrible idea," but "not because the notion of sponsoring an exile attempt to overthrow Castro seemed intolerable in itself." Such a reaction would be the merest sentimentality, unthinkable to a tough-minded realist. The difficulty, rather, was that it seemed unlikely that the deception could succeed. The operation, in his view, was ill-conceived but not otherwise objectionable. In a similar vein, Schlesinger quotes with approval Kennedy's "realistic" assessment of the situation resulting from Trujillo's assassination:

> There are three possibilities in descending order of preference: a decent democratic regime, a continuation of the Trujillo regime or a Castro regime. We ought to aim at the first, but we really can't renounce the second until we are sure that we can avoid the third. (*A Thousand Days: John F. Kennedy in the White House*, p. 769)

The reason why the third possibility is so intolerable is explained a few pages later (p. 774): "Communist success in Latin America would deal a much harder blow to the power and influence of the United States." Of course, we can never really be sure of avoiding the third possibility; therefore, in practice, we will always settle for the second, as we are now doing in Brazil and Argentina, for example. . . .

Let us, however, return to the war in Vietnam and the response that it has aroused among American intellectuals. A striking feature of the recent debate on Southeast Asian policy has been the distinction that is commonly drawn between "responsible criticism," on the one hand, and "sentimental," or "emotional," or "hysterical" criticism, on the other. There is much to be learned from a careful study of the terms in which this distinction is drawn. The "hysterical critics" are to be identified, apparently, by their irrational refusal to accept one fundamental political axiom, namely that the United States has the right to extend its power and control without limit, insofar as is feasible. Responsible criticism does not challenge this assumption, but argues, rather, that we probably can't "get away with it" at this particular time and place.

A distinction of this sort seems to be what Irving Kristol, for example, has in mind in his analysis of the protest over Vietnam policy (*Encounter*, August, 1965). He contrasts the responsible critics, such as Walter Lippmann, the *Times*, and Senator Fulbright, with the "teach-in movement." "Unlike the university protesters," he points out, "Mr. Lippmann engages in no presumptuous suppositions as to 'what the Vietnamese people really want'—he obviously doesn't much care—or in legalistic exegesis as to whether, or to what extent, there is 'aggression' or 'revolution' in South Vietnam. His is a *realpolitik* point of view; and he will apparently even contemplate the possibility of a *nuclear* war against China in extreme circumstances." This is commendable and contrasts favorably, for Kristol, with the talk of the "unreasonable, ideological types" in the teach-in movement, who often seem to be motivated by such absurdities as "simple, virtuous 'anti-imperialism,'" who deliver "harangues on 'the power structure,'" and who even sometimes stoop so low as to read "articles and reports from the foreign press on the American presence in Vietnam." Furthermore, these nasty types are often psychologists, mathematicians, chemists, or philosophers (just as, incidentally, those most vocal in protest in the Soviet Union are generally physicists, literary intellectuals, and others remote from the exercise of power), rather than people with Washington contacts, who, of course, realize that "had they a new, good idea about Vietnam, they would get a prompt and respectful hearing" in Washington.

I am not interested here in whether Kristol's characterization of protest and dissent is accurate, but rather in the assumptions on which it rests. Is the purity of American motives a matter that is beyond discussion, or that is irrelevant to discussion? Should decisions be left to "experts" with Washington contacts—even if we assume that they command the necessary knowledge and principles to make the "best" decision, will they invariably do so? And, a logically prior question, is "expertise" applicable—that is, is there a body of theory and of relevant information, not in the public domain, that can be applied to the analysis of foreign policy or that demonstrates the correctness of present actions in some way that psychologists, mathematicians, chemists, and philosophers are incapable of comprehending?

Although Kristol does not examine these questions directly, his attitude presupposes answers, answers which are wrong in all cases. American aggressiveness, however it may be masked in pious rhetoric, is a dominant force in world affairs and must be analyzed in terms of its causes and motives. There is no body of theory or significant body of relevant information, beyond the comprehension of the layman, which makes policy immune from criticism. To the extent that "expert knowledge" is applied to world affairs, it is surely appropriate—for a person of any integrity, quite necessary—to question its quality and the goals it serves. These facts seem too obvious to require extended discussion.

A corrective to Kristol's curious belief in the Administration's openness to new thinking about Vietnam is provided by McGeorge Bundy in a recent issue of *Foreign Affairs* (January, 1967). As Bundy correctly observes, "on the main stage . . . the argument on Viet Nam turns on tactics, not fundamentals," although, he adds, "there are wild men in the wings." On stage center are, of course, the President (who in his recent trip to Asia had just "magisterially reaffirmed" our interest "in the progress of the people across the Pacific") and his advisers, who deserve "the understanding support of those who want restraint." It is these men who deserve the credit for the fact that "the bombing of the North has been the most accurate and the most restrained in modern warfare"—a solicitude which will be appreciated by the inhabitants, or former inhabitants, of Nam Dinh and Phu Ly and Vinh. It is these men, too, who deserve the credit for what was reported by Malcolm Browne as long ago as May, 1965:

> In the South, huge sectors of the nation have been declared "free bombing zones," in which anything that moves is a legitimate target. Tens of thousands of tons of bombs, rockets, napalm and cannon fire are poured into these vast areas each week. If only by the laws of chance, bloodshed is believed to be heavy in these raids.

Fortunately for the developing countries, Bundy assures us, "American democracy has no taste for imperialism," and "taken as a whole, the stock of American experience, understanding, sympathy and simple knowledge is now much the most impressive in the world." It is true that "four-fifths of all the foreign investing in the world is now done by Americans" and that "the most admired plans and policies . . . are no better than their demonstrable relation to the American interest"—just as it is true, so we read in the same issue of *Foreign Affairs*, that the plans for armed action against Cuba were put into motion a few weeks after Mikoyan visited Havana, "invading what had so long been an almost exclusively American sphere of influence." Unfortunately, such facts as these are often taken by unsophisticated Asian intellectuals as indicating a "taste for imperialism." For example, a number of Indians have expressed their "near exasperation" at the fact that "we have done everything we can to attract foreign capital for fertilizer plants, but the American and the other Western private companies know we are over a barrel, so they demand stringent terms which we just cannot meet" (*Christian Science Monitor*, November 26), while "Washington . . . doggedly insists that deals be made in the private sector with private enterprise" (*ibid.*, December 5). But this reaction, no doubt, simply reveals, once again, how the Asian mind fails to comprehend the "diffuse and complex concepts" of Western thought. . . .

Having settled the issue of the political irrelevance of the protest movement, Kristol turns to the question of what motivates it—more generally, what has made students and junior faculty "go left," as he sees it, amid general prosperity and under liberal Welfare State administrations. This, he notes, "is a riddle to which no sociologist has as yet come up with an answer." Since these young people are well-off, have good futures, etc., their protest must be irrational. It must be the result of boredom, of too much security, or something of this sort. Other possibilities come to mind. It may be, for example, that as honest men the students and junior faculty are attempting to find out the truth for themselves rather than ceding the responsibility to "experts" or to government; and it may be that they react with indignation to what they discover. These possibilities Kristol does not reject. They are simply unthinkable, unworthy of consideration. More accurately, these possibilities are inexpressible; the categories in which they are formulated (honesty, indignation) simply do not exist for the tough-minded social scientist.

In this implicit disparagement of traditional intellectual values, Kristol reflects attitudes that are fairly widespread in academic circles. I do not doubt that these attitudes are in part a consequence of the desperate attempt of the social and behavioral sciences to imitate the surface features of sciences that really have significant intellectual content. But they have other sources as well. Anyone can be a moral individual, concerned with human rights and problems; but only a college professor, a trained expert, can solve technical problems by "sophisticated" methods. Ergo, it is only problems of the latter sort that are important or real. Responsible, non-ideological experts will give advice on tactical questions; irresponsible, "ideological types" will "harangue" about principle and trouble themselves over moral issues and human rights, or over the traditional problems of man and society, concerning which "social and behavioral science" has nothing to offer beyond trivialities. Obviously, these emotional, ideological types are irrational, since, being well-off and having power in their grasp, they shouldn't worry about such matters.

At times this pseudo-scientific posing reaches levels that are almost pathological. Consider the phenomenon of Herman Kahn, for example. Kahn has been both denounced as immoral and lauded for his courage. By people who should know better, his *On Thermonuclear War* has been described "without qualification . . . [as] . . . one of the great works of our time" (Stuart Hughes). The fact of the matter is that this is surely one of the emptiest works of our time, as can be seen by applying to it the intellectual standards of any existing discipline, by tracing some of its "well-documented conclusions" to the "objective studies" from which they derive, and by following the line of argument, where detectable. Kahn proposes no theories, no explanations, no factual assumptions that can be tested against their consequences, as do the sciences he is attempting to mimic. He simply suggests a terminology and provides a facade of rationality. When particular policy conclusions are drawn, they are supported only by *ex cathedra* remarks for which no support is even suggested (e.g., "The

civil defense line probably should be drawn somewhere below $5 bil-
lion annually" to keep from provoking the Russians—why not $50
billion, or $5.00?). What is more, Kahn is quite aware of this vacuity;
in his more judicious moments he claims only that "there is no reason to believe that relatively sophisticated models are more likely to
be misleading than the simpler models and analogies frequently used
as an aid to judgment." For those whose humor tends towards the
macabre, it is easy to play the game of "strategic thinking" *à la* Kahn,
and to prove what one wishes. For example, one of Kahn's basic assumptions is that

> an all-out surprise attack in which all resources are devoted to counter-
> value targets would be so irrational that, barring an incredible lack of
> sophistication or actual insanity among Soviet decision makers, such
> an attack is highly unlikely.

A simple argument proves the opposite. *Premise 1:* American
decision-makers think along the lines outlined by Herman Kahn.
Premise 2: Kahn thinks it would be better for everyone to be red than
for everyone to be dead. *Premise 3*: if the Americans were to respond
to an all-out countervalue attack, then everyone would be dead. *Conclusion*: the Americans will not respond to an all-out countervalue
attack, and therefore it should be launched without delay. Of course,
one can carry the argument a step further. *Fact*: the Russians have
not carried out an all-out countervalue attack. It follows that they
are not rational. If they are not rational, there is no point in "strategic thinking." Therefore, . . .

Of course this is all nonsense, but nonsense that differs from
Kahn's only in the respect that the argument is of slightly greater
complexity than anything to be discovered in his work. What is re-
markable is that serious people actually pay attention to these absurdities, no doubt because of the facade of tough-mindedness and
pseudo-science. . . .

A good case can be made for the conclusion that there is indeed
something of a consensus among intellectuals who have already

achieved power and affluence, or who sense that they can achieve them by "accepting society" as it is and promoting the values that are "being honored" in this society. It is also true that this consensus is most noticeable among the scholar-experts who are replacing the free-floating intellectuals of the past. In the university, these scholar-experts construct a "value-free technology" for the solution of technical problems that arise in contemporary society, taking a "responsible stance" towards these problems, in the sense noted earlier. This consensus among the responsible scholar-experts is the domestic analogue to that proposed, internationally, by those who justify the application of American power in Asia, whatever the human cost, on the grounds that it is necessary to contain the "expansion of China" (an "expansion" which is, to be sure, hypothetical for the time being)—that is, to translate from State Department Newspeak, on the grounds that it is essential to reverse the Asian nationalist revolutions or, at least, to prevent them from spreading. The analogy becomes clear when we look carefully at the ways in which this proposal is formulated. With his usual lucidity, Churchill outlined the general position in a remark to his colleague of the moment, Joseph Stalin, at Teheran in 1943:

> The government of the world must be entrusted to satisfied nations, who wished nothing more for themselves than what they had. If the world-government were in the hands of hungry nations there would always be danger. But none of us had any reason to seek for anything more. . . . Our power placed us above the rest. We were like the rich men dwelling at peace within their habitations.

For a translation of Churchill's biblical rhetoric into the jargon of contemporary social science, one may turn to the testimony of Charles Wolf, Senior Economist of the Rand Corporation, at the Congressional Committee Hearings:

> I am dubious that China's fears of encirclement are going to be abated, eased, relaxed in the long-term future. But I would hope that what we do in Southeast Asia would help to develop within the Chinese body

> politic more of a realism and willingness to live with this fear than to indulge it by support for liberation movements, which admittedly depend on a great deal more than external support . . . the operational question for American foreign policy is not whether that fear can be eliminated or substantially alleviated, but whether China can be faced with a structure of incentives, of penalties and rewards, of inducements that will make it willing to live with this fear.

The point is further clarified by Thomas Schelling: "There is growing experience, which the Chinese can profit from, that although the United States may be interested in encircling them, may be interested in defending nearby areas from them, it is, nevertheless, prepared to behave peaceably if they are."

In short, we are prepared to live peaceably in our—to be sure, rather extensive—habitations. And, quite naturally, we are offended by the undignified noises from the servants' quarters. If, let us say, a peasant-based revolutionary movement tries to achieve independence from foreign powers and the domestic structures they support, or if the Chinese irrationally refuse to respond properly to the schedule of reinforcement that we have prepared for them—if they object to being encircled by the benign and peace-loving "rich men" who control the territories on their borders as a natural right—then, evidently, we must respond to this belligerence with appropriate force.

It is this mentality that explains the frankness with which the United States Government and its academic apologists defend the American refusal to permit a political settlement in Vietnam at a local level, a settlement based on the actual distribution of political forces. Even government experts freely admit that the NLF is the only "truly mass-based political party in South Vietnam" (Douglas Pike, *Viet Cong*); that the NLF had "made a conscious and massive effort to extend political participation, even if it was manipulated, on the local level so as to involve the people in a self-contained, self-supporting revolution" (p. 374); and that this effort had been so successful that no political groups, "with the possible exception of the Buddhists, thought themselves equal in size and power to risk entering into a

coalition, fearing that if they did the whale would swallow the min-
now" (p. 362). Moreover, they concede that until the introduction of
overwhelming American force, the NLF had insisted that the struggle "should be fought out at the political level and that the use of
massed military might was in itself illegitimate. . . . The battleground
was to be the minds and loyalties of the rural Vietnamese, the weapons were to be ideas" (pp. 91–92; cf. also pp. 93, 99–108, 155f.); and,
correspondingly, that until mid-1964, aid from Hanoi "was largely
confined to two areas—doctrinal know-how and leadership personnel" (p. 321). Captured NLF documents contrast the enemy's "military superiority" with their own "political superiority" (p. 106), thus
fully confirming the analysis of American military spokesmen who
define our problem as how, "with considerable armed force but little
political power, [to] contain an adversary who has enormous political force but only modest military power" (Jean Lacouture, *Vietnam
Between Two Truces*).

Similarly, the most striking outcome of both the Honolulu conference in February and the Manila conference in October was the
frank admission by high officials of the Saigon government that
"they could not survive a 'peaceful settlement' that left the Vietcong
political structure in place even if the Vietcong guerilla units were dis-
banded," that "they are not able to compete *politically* with the Vietnamese Communists" (Charles Mohr, *New York Times*, February 11,
1966, italics mine). Thus, Mohr continues, the Vietnamese demand a
"pacification program" which will have as "its core . . . the destruction of the clandestine Vietcong political structure and the creation of
an iron-like system of government political control over the population." And from Manila, the same correspondent, on October 23,
quotes a high South Vietnamese official as saying that:

> Frankly, we are not strong enough now to compete with the Commu-
> nists on a purely political basis. They are organized and disciplined.
> The non-Communist nationalists are not—we do not have any large,
> well-organized political parties and we do not yet have unity. We can-
> not leave the Vietcong in existence.

Officials in Washington understand the situation very well. Thus Secretary Rusk has pointed out that "if the Vietcong come to the conference table as full partners they will, in a sense, have been victorious in the very aims that South Vietnam and the United States are pledged to prevent" (January 28, 1966). Max Frankel reported from Washington in the *Times* on February 18, 1966, that

> Compromise has had no appeal here because the Administration concluded long ago that the non-Communist forces of South Vietnam could not long survive in a Saigon coalition with Communists. It is for that reason—and not because of an excessively rigid sense of protocol—that Washington has steadfastly refused to deal with the Vietcong or recognize them as an independent political force.

In short, we will—magnanimously—permit Vietcong representatives to attend negotiations only if they will agree to identify themselves as agents of a foreign power and thus forfeit the right to participate in a coalition government, a right which they have now been demanding for a half-dozen years. We well know that in any representative coalition, our chosen delegates could not last a day without the support of American arms. Therefore, we must increase American force and resist meaningful negotiations, until the day when a client government can exert both military and political control over its own population—a day which may never dawn, for as William Bundy has pointed out, we could never be sure of the security of a Southeast Asia "from which the Western presence was effectively withdrawn." Thus if we were to "negotiate in the direction of solutions that are put under the label of neutralization," this would amount to capitulation to the Communists. According to this reasoning, then, South Vietnam must remain, permanently, an American military base.

All of this is, of course, reasonable, so long as we accept the fundamental political axiom that the United States, with its traditional concern for the rights of the weak and downtrodden, and with its unique insight into the proper mode of development for backward countries, must have the courage and the persistence to impose its will by force until such time as other nations are prepared to accept these truths—or simply, to abandon hope.

If it is the responsibility of the intellectual to insist upon the truth, it is also his duty to see events in their historical perspective. Thus one must applaud the insistence of the Secretary of State on the importance of historical analogies, the Munich analogy, for example. As Munich showed, a powerful and aggressive nation with a fanatic belief in its manifest destiny will regard each victory, each extension of its power and authority, as a prelude to the next step. The matter was very well put by Adlai Stevenson, when he spoke of "the old, old route whereby expansive powers push at more and more doors, believing they will open until, at the ultimate door, resistance is unavoidable and major war breaks out." Herein lies the danger of appeasement, as the Chinese tirelessly point out to the Soviet Union—which, they claim, is playing Chamberlain to our Hitler in Vietnam. Of course, the aggressiveness of liberal imperialism is not that of Nazi Germany, though the distinction may seem academic to a Vietnamese peasant who is being gassed or incinerated. We do not want to occupy Asia; we merely wish, to return to Mr. Wolf, "to help the Asian countries progress toward economic modernization, as relatively 'open' and stable societies, to which our access, as a country and as individual citizens, is free and comfortable." The formulation is appropriate. Recent history shows that it makes little difference to us what form of government a country has so long as it remains an "open society," in our peculiar sense of this term—that is, a society that remains open to American economic penetration or political control. If it is necessary to approach genocide in Vietnam to achieve this objective, than this is the price we must pay in defense of freedom and the rights of man.

In pursuing the aim of helping other countries to progress toward open societies, with no thought of territorial aggrandizement, we are breaking no new ground. In the Congressional Hearings [. . .] Hans Morgenthau aptly describes our traditional policy towards China as one which favors "what you might call freedom of competition with regard to the exploitation of China." In fact, few imperialist powers have had explicit territorial ambitions. Thus in 1784, the British Parliament announced: "To pursue schemes of conquest and extension of dominion in India are measures repugnant to the wish, honor, and policy of this nation." Shortly after this, the conquest of India was in full swing. A century later, Britain announced its intentions in Egypt under the slogan "intervention, reform, withdrawal." It is obvious which parts of this promise were fulfilled within the next half-century. In 1936, on the eve of hostilities in North China, the Japanese stated their Basic Principles of National Policy. These included the use of moderate and peaceful means to extend her strength, to promote social and economic development, to eradicate the menace of Communism, to correct the aggressive policies of the great powers, and to secure her position as the stabilizing power in East Asia. Even in 1937, the Japanese government had "no territorial designs upon China." In short, we follow a well-trodden path.

It is useful to remember, incidentally, that the United States was apparently quite willing, as late as 1939, to negotiate a commercial treaty with Japan and arrive at a *modus vivendi* if Japan would "change her attitude and practice towards our rights and interests in China," as Secretary Hull put it. The bombing of Chungking and the rape of Nanking were unpleasant, it is true, but what was really important was our rights and interests in China, as the responsible, unhysterical men of the day saw quite clearly. It was the closing of the open door by Japan that led inevitably to the Pacific war, just as it is the closing of the open door by "Communist" China itself that may very well lead to the next, and no doubt last, Pacific war.

Quite often, the statements of sincere and devoted technical experts give surprising insight into the intellectual attitudes that lie in the background of the latest savagery. Consider, for example, the following comment by the economist Richard Lindholm, in 1959, expressing his frustration over the failure of economic development in "free Vietnam":

> . . . the use of American aid is determined by how the Vietnamese use
> their incomes and their savings. The fact that a large portion of the

Vietnamese imports financed with American aid are either consumer goods or raw materials used rather directly to meet consumer demands is an indication that the Vietnamese people desire these goods, for they have shown their desire by their willingness to use their piasters to purchase them. (*Vietnam: The First Five Years*)

In short, the Vietnamese *people* desire Buicks and air-conditioners, rather than sugar refining equipment or road-building machinery, as they have shown by their behavior in a free market. And however much we may deplore their free choice, we must allow the people to have their way. Of course, there are also those two-legged beasts of burden that one stumbles on in the countryside, but as any graduate student of political science can explain, they are not part of a responsible modernizing elite, and therefore have only a superficial biological resemblance to the human race.

In no small measure, it is attitudes like this that lie behind the butchery in Vietnam, and we had better face up to them with candor, or we will find our government leading us towards a "final solution" in Vietnam, and in the many Vietnams that inevitably lie ahead.

Let me finally return to Dwight Macdonald and the responsibility of intellectuals. Macdonald quotes an interview with a death-camp paymaster who burst into tears when told that the Russians would hang him. "Why should they? What have I done?" he asked. Macdonald concludes: "Only those who are willing to resist authority themselves when it conflicts too intolerably with their personal moral code, only they have the right to condemn the death-camp paymaster." The question, "What have I done?" is one that we may well ask ourselves, as we read each day of fresh atrocities in Vietnam—as we create, or mouth, or tolerate the deceptions that will be used to justify the next defense of freedom.

22. KATE MILLETT

Sexual Politics: A Manifesto for Revolution
(1970)

KATE MILLETT's "Sexual Politics: A Manifesto for Revolution" succinctly described the rationale and the goals of the women's liberation movement. Millett (1937–) was born in St. Paul, Minnesota, and she earned her Ph.D. from Columbia University in 1970. Her dissertation, published in book form as *Sexual Politics*, became a national best-seller and quickly made Millett a prominent figure in the women's liberation movement. She has also written several memoirs and books on various social ills. "Sexual Politics: A Manifesto for Revolution" posited a social movement that would promote sexual freedom and allow for women to attain "full human status after millennia of deprivation and oppression."

SOURCE: Shulamith Firestone and Anne Koedt. *Notes from the Second Year.* New York: Radical Feminism, 1970.

SELECT BIBLIOGRAPHY: Jeanne Martha Perreault, *Writing Selves: Contemporary Feminist Autobiography* (1995). Kate Millett, *Flying* (1974). Kate Millett, *Sexual Politics* (1970).

When one group rules another, the relationship between the two is political. When such an arrangement is carried out over a long period of time, it develops an ideology (feudalism, racism, etc.). All historical civilizations are patriarchies: their ideology is male supremacy.

Oppressed groups are denied education, economic independence, the power of office, representation, an image of dignity and self-respect, equality of status, and recognition as human beings. Throughout history women have been consistently denied all of these, and their denial today, while attenuated and partial, is nevertheless consistent. The education allowed them is deliberately designed to be inferior, and they are systematically programmed out of and excluded from the knowledge where power lies today—e.g., in science and technology. They are confined to conditions of economic dependence based on the sale of their sexuality in marriage, or a variety of prostitutions. Work on a basis of economic independence allows them only a subsistence level of life— often not even that. They do not hold office, are represented in no positions of power, and authority is forbidden them. The image of women fostered by cultural media, high and low, then and now, is a marginal and demeaning existence, and one outside the human condition— which is defined as the prerogative of man, the male.

Government is upheld by power, which is supported through consent (social opinion), or imposed by violence. Conditioning to an ideology amounts to the former. But there may be a resort to the latter at any moment when consent is withdrawn—rape, attack, sequestration, beatings, murder. Sexual politics obtains consent through the "socialization" of both sexes to patriarchal policies. They consist of the following:

1) the formation of human personality along stereotyped lines of sexual category, based on the needs and values of the master class and dictated by what he would cherish in himself and find convenient in an underclass: aggression, intellectuality, force, and efficiency for the male; passivity, ignorance, docility, "virtue," and ineffectuality for the female.

2) the concept of sex role, which assigns domestic service and attendance upon infants to all females and the rest of human interest, achievement and ambition to the male; the charge of leader at all times and places to the male, and the duty of follower, with equal uniformity, to the female.

3) the imposition of male rule through institutions: patriarchal

religion, the proprietary family, marriage, "The Home," masculine oriented culture, and a pervasive doctrine of male superiority.

A Sexual Revolution would bring about the following conditions, desirable upon rational, moral and humanistic grounds:

1) the end of sexual repression—freedom of expression and of sexual mores (sexual freedom has been partially attained, but it is now being subverted beyond freedom into exploitative license for patriarchal and reactionary ends).

2) Unisex, or the end of separatist character-structure, temperament and behavior, so that each individual may develop an entire— rather than a partial, limited, and conformist—personality.

3) re-examination of traits categorized into "masculine" and "feminine," with a total reassessment as to their human usefulness and advisability in both sexes. Thus if "masculine" violence is undesirable, it is so for both sexes; "feminine" dumb-cow passivity likewise. If "masculine" intelligence or efficiency is valuable, it is so for both sexes equally, and the same must be true for "feminine" tenderness or consideration.

4) the end of sex role and sex status, the patriarchy and the male supremacist ethic, attitude and ideology—in all areas of endeavor, experience, and behavior.

5) the end of the ancient oppression of the young under the patriarchal proprietary family, their chattel status, the attainment of the human rights presently denied them, the professionalization and therefore improvement of their care, and the guarantee that when they enter the world, they are desired, planned for, and provided with equal opportunities.

6) Bisex, or the end of enforced perverse heterosexuality, so that the sex act ceases to be arbitrarily polarized into male and female, to the exclusion of sexual expression between members of the same sex.

7) the end of sexuality in the forms in which it has existed historically—brutality, violence, capitalism, exploitation, and warfare— that it may cease to be hatred and become love.

8) the attainment of the female sex to freedom and full human status after millennia of deprivation and oppression, and of both sexes to a viable humanity.

23. CARL WITTMAN

Refugees from Amerika: A Gay Manifesto
(1970)

CARL WITTMAN's "Refugees from Amerika: A Gay Manifesto" was a flagship document in the gay liberation movement. Wittman (1943–1986) was born and raised in New Jersey and was active in the Civil Rights Movement and Students for a Democratic Society (SDS) while he attended Swarthmore College. In 1967 he moved to San Francisco, where he worked as a labor organizer. Although published for the first time in December 1970, Wittman's "Refugees from Amerika: A Gay Manifesto" was actually written shortly before the Stonewall Rebellion, and it was well received in the underground press because it drew together many of the early themes of gay liberation. Wittman called for a rejection of heterosexual standards and a politics of open confrontation that aimed to radically transform all of society.

SOURCE: Joseph A. McCaffrey. *The Homosexual Dialectic.* Englewood Cliffs, New Jersey: Prentice Hall, 1972.

SELECTED READINGS: Barry Adam, *The Rise of a Gay and Lesbian Movement* (1987). Donn Teal, *The Gay Militants: How Gay Liberation Began in America, 1969–1971* (1971). Karla Jay and Allen Young, *Out of the Closets: Voices of Gay Liberation* (1972).

San Francisco is a refugee camp for homosexuals. We have fled here from every part of the nation, and like refugees elsewhere, we came not because it is so great here, but because it was so bad there. By the tens of thousands, we fled small towns where to be ourselves would endanger our jobs and any hope of a decent life; we have fled from blackmailing cops, from families who disowned or "tolerated" us; we have been drummed out of the armed services, thrown out of schools, fired from jobs, beaten by punks and policemen.

And we have formed a ghetto, out of self-protection. It is a ghetto rather than a free territory because it is still theirs. Straight cops patrol us, straight legislators govern us, straight employers keep us in line, straight money exploits us. We have pretended everything is OK, because we haven't been able to see how to change it—we've been afraid.

In the past year there has been an awakening of gay liberation ideas and energy. How it began we don't know; maybe we were inspired by black people and their freedom movement; we learned how to stop pretending from the hip revolution. Amerika in all its ugliness has surfaced with the war and our national leaders. And we are revulsed by the quality of our ghetto life.

Where once there was frustration, alienation, and cynicism, there are new characteristics among us. We are full of love for each other and are showing it; we are full of anger at what has been done to us. And as we recall all the self-censorship and repression for so many years, a reservoir of tears pours out of our eyes. And we are euphoric, high, with the initial flourish of a movement.

We want to make ourselves clear: our first job is to free ourselves; that means clearing our heads of the garbage that's been poured into them. This article is an attempt at raising a number of issues and presenting some ideas to replace the old ones. It is primarily for ourselves a starting point of discussion. If straight people of good will find it useful in understanding what liberation is about, so much the better.

It should also be clear that these are the views of one person, and are determined not only by my homosexuality, but my being white, male, middle-class. It is my individual consciousness. Our group consciousness will evolve as we get ourselves together—we are only at the beginning.

I. On Orientation

1. *What homosexuality is:* Nature leaves undefined the object of sexual desire. The gender of that object is imposed socially. Humans originally made homosexuality taboo because they needed every bit of energy to produce and raise children: survival of species was a priority. With overpopulation and technological change, that taboo continued only to exploit us and enslave us.

As kids we refused to capitulate to demands that we ignore our feelings toward each other. Somewhere we found the strength to resist being indoctrinated, and we should count that among our assets. We have to realize that our loving each other is a good thing, not an unfortunate thing, and that we have a lot to teach straights about sex, love, strength, and resistance.

Homosexuality is *not* a lot of things. It is not a makeshift in the absence of the opposite sex; it is not hatred or rejection of the opposite sex; it is not genetic; it is not the result of broken homes except inasmuch as we could see the sham of American marriage. *Homosexuality is the capacity to love someone of the same sex.*

2. *Bisexuality:* Bisexuality is good; it is the capacity to love people of either sex. The reason so few of us are bisexual is because society made such a big stink about homosexuality that we got forced into seeing ourselves as either straight or non-straight. Also, many gays got turned off to the ways men are supposed to act with women and vice-versa, which is pretty fucked-up. Gays will begin to turn on to women when 1) it's something that we do because we want to and not because we should, and 2) when women's liberation changes the nature of heterosexual relationships.

We continue to call ourselves homosexual, not bisexual, even if we do make it with the opposite sex also, because saying "Oh, I'm Bi" is a copout for a gay. We get told it's OK to sleep with guys as long as we sleep with women too, and that's still putting homosexuality down. We'll be gay until everyone has forgotten that it's an issue. Then we'll begin to be complete.

3. *Heterosexuality:* Exclusive heterosexuality is fucked up. It reflects a fear of people of the same sex, it's anti-homosexual, and it is fraught with frustration. Heterosexual sex is fucked up, too; ask women's liberation about what straight guys are like in bed. Sex is aggression for the male chauvinist; sex is obligation for the traditional woman. And among the young, the modern, the hip, it's only a subtle version of the same. For us to become heterosexual in the sense that our straight brothers and sisters are is not a cure, it is a disease. . . .

III. On Roles

1. *Mimicry of straight society:* We are children of straight society. We still think straight: that is part of our oppression. One of the worst of straight concepts is inequality. Straight (also white, English, male, capitalist) thinking views things in terms of order and comparison. A is before B, B is after A; one is below two is below three; there is no room for equality. This idea gets extended to male/female, on top/on bottom, spouse/not spouse, heterosexual/homosexual, boss/worker, white/black, and rich/poor. Our social institutions cause and reflect this verbal hierarchy. This is Amerika.

We've lived in these institutions all our lives. Naturally we mimic the roles. For too long we mimicked these roles to protect ourselves—a survival mechanism. Now we are becoming free enough to shed the roles which we've picked up from the institutions which have imprisoned us.

"Stop mimicking straights, stop censoring ourselves."

2. *Marriage:* Marriage is a prime example of a straight institution fraught with role playing. Traditional marriage is a rotten, oppressive institution. Those of us who have been in heterosexual marriages too often have blamed our gayness on the breakup of the marriage. No. They broke up because marriage is a contract which smothers both people, denies needs, and places impossible demands on both people.

And we had the strength, again, to refuse to capitulate to the roles which were demanded of us.

Gay people must stop gauging their self-respect by how well they mimic straight marriages. Gay marriages will have the same problems as straight ones except in burlesque. For the usual legitimacy and pressures which keep straight marriages together are absent, e.g., kids, what parents think, what neighbors say.

To accept that happiness comes through finding a groovy spouse and settling down, showing the world that "we're just the same as you" is avoiding the real issues and is an expression of self-hatred.

3. *Alternatives to marriage:* People want to get married for lots of good reasons, although marriage won't often meet those needs or desires. We're all looking for security, a flow of love, and a feeling of belonging and being needed.

These needs can be met through a number of social relationships and living situations. Things we want to get away from are: 1) Exclusiveness, propertied attitudes toward each other, a mutual pact against the rest of the world; 2) Promises about the future, which we have no right to make and which prevent us from, or make us feel guilty about, growing; 3) Inflexible roles, roles which do not reflect us at the moment but are inherited through mimicry and inability to define equalitarian relationships.

We have to define for ourselves a new pluralistic, role-free social structure for ourselves. It must contain both the freedom and physical space for people to live alone, live together for a while, live together for a long time, either as couples or in larger numbers, and the ability to flow easily from one of these states to another as our needs change.

Liberation for gay people is defining for ourselves how and with whom we live, instead of measuring our relationship in comparison to straight ones, with straight values.

4. *Gay "stereotypes":* The straights' image of the gay world is defined largely by those of us who have violated straight roles. There is a tendency among "homophile" groups to deplore gays who play visible roles—the queens and the nellies. As liberated gays, we must take a clear stand. 1) Gays who stand out have become our first martyrs. They came out and withstood disapproval before the rest of us did. 2)

If they have suffered from being open, it is straight society whom we must indict, not the queen.

5. *Closet queens:* This phrase is becoming analagous to "Uncle Tom." To pretend to be straight sexually, or to pretend to be straight socially, is probably the most harmful pattern of behavior in the ghetto. The married guy who makes it on the side secretly; the guy who will go to bed once but who won't develop any gay relationships; the pretender at work or school who changes the gender of the friend he's talking about; the guy who'll suck cock in the bushes but who won't go to bed.

If we are liberated, we are open with our sexuality. Closet queenery must end. *Come out.*

But in saying come out, we have to have our heads clear about a few things: 1) Closet queens are our brothers and must be defended against attacks by straight people. 2) The fear of coming out is not paranoia; the stakes are high: loss of family ties, loss of job, loss of straight friends—these are all reminders that the oppression is not just in our heads. It's real. Each of us must make the steps toward openness at our own speed and on our own impulses. Being open is the foundation of freedom: it has to be built solidly. 3) "Closet queen" is a broad term covering a multitude of forms of defense, self-hatred, lack of strength, and habit. We are all closet queens in some ways, and all of us had to come out—very few of us were "flagrant" at the age of seven! We must afford our brothers and sisters the same patience we afforded ourselves. And while their closet queenery is part of our oppression, it's more a part of theirs. They alone can decide when and how.

IV. On Oppression

It is important to catalog and understand the different facets of our oppression. There is no future in arguing about degrees of oppression. A lot of "movement" types come on with a line of shit about homosexuals not being oppressed as much as blacks or Vietnamese or workers or women. We don't happen to fit into their ideas of class or caste. Bull! When people feel oppressed, they act on that feeling. We feel oppressed.

Talk about the priority of black liberation or ending imperialism over and above gay liberation is just anti-gay propaganda.

1. *Physical attacks:* We are attacked, beaten, castrated and left dead time and time again. There are half a dozen known unsolved slayings in San Francisco parks in the last few years. "Punks," often of minority groups who look around for someone under them socially, feel encouraged to beat up on "queens," and cops look the other way. That used to be called lynching.

Cops in most cities have harassed our meeting places: bars and baths and parks. They set up entrapment squads. A Berkeley brother was slain by a cop in April when he tried to split after finding out that the trick who was making advances to him was a cop. Cities set up "pervert" registration, which if nothing else scares our brothers deeper into the closet.

One of the most vicious slurs on us is the blame for prison "gang rapes." These rapes are invariably done by people who consider themselves straight. The victims of these rapes are us and straights who can't defend themselves. The press campaign to link prison rapes with homosexuality is an attempt to make straights fear and despise us, so they can oppress us more. It's typical of the fucked-up straight mind to think that homosexual sex involves tying a guy down and fucking him. That's aggression, not sex. If that's what sex is for a lot of straight people, that's a problem they have to solve, not us.

2. *Psychological warfare:* Right from the beginning we have been subjected to a barrage of straight propaganda. Since our parents don't know any homosexuals, we grow up thinking that we're alone and different and perverted. Our school friends identify "queer" with any non-conformist or bad behavior. Our elementary school teachers tell us not to talk to strangers or accept rides. Television, billboards and magazines put forth a false idealization of male/female relationships and make us wish we were different, wish we were "in." In family living class we're taught how we're supposed to turn out. And all along the best we hear about homosexuality is that it's an unfortunate problem.

3. *Self-oppression:* As gay liberation grows, we will find our uptight brothers and sisters, particularly those who are making a buck off

our ghetto, coming on strong to defend the status quo. This is self-oppression: "don't rock the boat"; "things in SF are OK"; "gay people just aren't together"; "I'm not oppressed." These lines are right out of the mouths of the straight establishment. A large part of our oppression would end if we would stop putting ourselves and our pride down.

4. *Institutional oppression:* Discrimination against gays is blatant, if we open our eyes. Homosexual relationships are illegal, and even if these laws are not regularly enforced, they encourage and enforce closet queenery. The bulk of the social work/psychiatric field looks upon homosexuality as a problem, and treats us as sick. Employers let it be known that our skills are acceptable only as long as our sexuality is hidden. Big business and government are particularly notorious offenders.

The discrimination in the draft and armed services is a pillar of the general attitude toward gays. If we are willing to label ourselves publicly not only as homosexual but as sick, then we qualify for deferment; and if we're not "discreet" (dishonest) we get drummed out of the service. Hell, no, we won't go, of course not, but we can't let the army fuck us over this way, either. . . .

VI. On Our Ghetto

We are refugees from Amerika. So we came to the ghetto—and as other ghettos, it has its negative and positive aspects. Refugee camps are better than what proceeded them, or people never would have come. But they are still enslaving, if only that we are limited to being ourselves there and only there.

Ghettos breed self-hatred. We stagnate here, accepting the status quo. The status quo is rotten. We are all warped by our oppression, and in the isolation of the ghetto we blame ourselves rather than our oppressors.

Ghettos breed exploitation. Landlords find they can charge exorbitant rents, and get away with it, because of the limited area which is safe to live in openly. Mafia control of bars and baths in NYC is only one example of outside money controlling our institutions for their profit. In San Francisco the Tavern Guild favors maintaining the ghetto, for it is through ghetto culture that they make a buck. We crowd their bars not because of their merit but because of the absence of any other social institution. The Guild has refused to let us collect defense funds or pass out gay liberation literature in their bars—need we ask why?

Police or con men who shake down the straight gay in return for not revealing him; the bookstores and movie makers who keep raising prices because they are the only outlet for pornography; heads of "modeling" agencies and other pimps who exploit both the hustlers and the johns—these are the parasites who flourish in the ghetto.

San Francisco—ghetto or free territory? Our ghetto certainly is more beautiful and larger and more diverse than most ghettos, and is certainly freer than the rest of Amerika. That's why we're here. But it isn't ours. Capitalists make money off us, cops patrol us, government tolerates us as long as we shut up, and daily we work for and pay taxes to those who oppress us.

To be a free territory, we must govern ourselves, set up our own institutions, defend ourselves, and use our own energies to improve our lives. The emergence of gay liberation communes and our own paper is a good start. The talk about a gay liberation coffee shop/dance hall should be acted upon. Rural retreats, political action offices, food cooperatives, a free school, unalienating bars and after hours places— they must be developed if we are to have even the shadow of a free territory. . . .

Conclusion: An Outline of Imperatives for Gay Liberation

1. Free ourselves: come out everywhere; initiate self defense and political activity; initiate counter-community institutions.

2. Turn other gay people on: talk all the time; understand, forgive, accept.

3. Free the homosexual in everyone: we'll be getting a good bit of shit from threatened latents: be gentle, and keep talking and acting free.

4. We've been playing an act for a long time, so we're consummate actors. Now we can begin to be, and it'll be a good show!

24. ANGELA Y. DAVIS

Political Prisoners, Prisons,
and Black Liberation
(1971)

ANGELA DAVIS's "Political Prisoners, Prisons, and Black Liberation" called for a unified struggle against the onset of racism and fascism in the United States. Because of her affiliation with the Communist Party, U.S.A., Davis (1944–) was dismissed from her teaching position at the University of California, Los Angeles, in 1969. In 1970 she was charged with kidnapping, conspiracy, and murder for her role in connection with a courtroom shootout that resulted from an attempt to free Black Panther George Jackson. Her trial was a cause célèbre, and she was acquitted of all charges. She has continued to champion numerous progressive causes and is currently a professor in the History of Consciousness program at the University of California, Santa Cruz. As the essay below suggests, Davis has been particularly outspoken against the prison-industrial complex, and she has been a staunch advocate for political prisoners in the United States.

SOURCE: Angela Y. Davis, ed., *If They Come in the Morning: Voices of Resistance.* New York: Third Press, 1971.

SELECTED READINGS: *The Angela Y. Davis Reader*, ed. Joy James (1998). Angela Y. Davis, *Angela Davis: An Autobiography* (1988). Bettina Aptheker, *The Morning Breaks: The Trial of Angela Davis* (1975).

Despite a long history of exalted appeals to man's inherent right of resistance, there has seldom been agreement on how to relate in *practice* to unjust, immoral laws and the oppressive social order from which they emanate.* The conservative, who does not dispute the validity of revolutions deeply buried in history, invokes visions of impending anarchy in order to legitimize his demand for absolute obedience. Law and order, with the major emphasis on order, is his watchword. The liberal articulates his sensitivity to certain of society's intolerable details, but will almost never prescribe methods of resistance that exceed the limits of legality—redress through electoral channels is the liberal's panacea.

In the heat of our pursuit of fundamental human rights, black people have been continually cautioned to be patient. We are advised that as long as we remain faithful to the *existing* democratic order, the glorious moment will eventually arrive when we will come into our own as full-fledged human beings.

But having been taught by bitter experience, we know that there is a glaring incongruity between democracy and the capitalist economy which is the source of our ills. Regardless of all rhetoric to the contrary, the people are not the ultimate matrix of the laws and the system which govern them—certainly not black people and other nationally oppressed people, but not even the mass of whites. The people do not exercise decisive control over the determining factors of their lives.

Official assertions that meaningful dissent is always welcome, provided it falls within the boundaries of legality, are frequently a smokescreen obscuring the invitation to acquiesce in oppression. Slavery may have been unrighteous, the constitutional provision for the enslavement of blacks may have been unjust, but conditions were not to be considered so unbearable (especially since they were profitable to a small circle) as to justify escape and other acts proscribed by law. This was the import of the fugitive slave laws.

Author's note, 1998: I have opted to leave masculinist formulations in this and other early essays, which I hope will be considered in the context of the historical period in which they were produced.

Needless to say, the history of the United States has been marred from its inception by an enormous quantity of unjust laws, far too many expressly bolstering the oppression of black people. Particularized reflections of existing social inequities, these laws have repeatedly borne witness to the exploitative and racist core of the society itself: For blacks, Chicanos, for all nationally oppressed people, the problem of opposing unjust laws and the social conditions which nourish their growth, has always had immediate practical implications. Our very survival has frequently been a direct function of our skill in forging effective channels of resistance. In resisting we have sometimes been compelled to openly violate those laws which directly or indirectly buttress our oppression. But even when containing our resistance within the orbit of legality, we have been labeled criminals and have been methodically persecuted by a racist legal apparatus. . . .

The prison is a key component of the state's coercive apparatus, the overriding function of which is to ensure social control. The etymology of the term "penitentiary" furnishes a clue to the controlling idea behind the "prison system" at its inception. The penitentiary was projected as the locale for doing penitence for an offense against society, the physical and spiritual purging of proclivities to challenge rules and regulations which command total obedience. While cloaking itself with the bourgeois aura of universality—imprisonment was supposed to cut across all class lines, as crimes were to be defined by the act, not the perpetrator—the prison has actually operated as an instrument of class domination, a means of prohibiting the have-nots from encroaching upon the haves.

The occurrence of crime is inevitable in a society in which wealth is unequally distributed, as one of the constant reminders that society's productive forces are being channeled in the wrong direction. The majority of criminal offenses bear a direct relationship to property. Contained in the very concept of property, crimes are profound but suppressed social needs which express themselves in anti-social modes of action. Spontaneously produced by a capitalist organization of society, this type of crime is at once a protest against society and a desire to partake of its exploitative content. It challenges the symptoms of capitalism, but not its essence. . . .

Especially today when so many black, Chicano, and Puerto Rican men and women are jobless as a consequence of the internal dynamic of the capitalist system, the role of the unemployed, which includes the lumpenproletariat in revolutionary struggle, must be given serious thought. Increased unemployment, particularly for the nationally oppressed, will continue to be an inevitable by-product of technological development. At least 30 percent of black youth are presently without jobs. [In 1997, over 30 percent of young black men were in prison, on probation or on parole.] In the context of class exploitation and national oppression it should be clear that numerous individuals are compelled to resort to criminal acts, not as a result of conscious choice—implying other alternatives—but because society has objectively reduced their possibilities of subsistence and survival to this level. This recognition should signal the urgent need to organize the unemployed and lumpenproletariat, as indeed the Black Panther Party as well as activists in prison have already begun to do.

In evaluating the susceptibility of the black and brown unemployed to organizing efforts, the peculiar historical features of the United States, specifically racism and national oppression, must be taken into account. There already exists in the black and brown communities, the lumpenproletariat included, a long tradition of collective resistance to national oppression.

Moreover, in assessing the revolutionary potential of prisoners in America as a group, it should be borne in mind that not all prisoners have actually committed crimes. The built-in racism of the judicial system expresses itself, as Du Bois has suggested, in the railroading of countless innocent blacks and other national minorities into the country's coercive institutions.

One must also appreciate the effects of disproportionally long prison terms on black and brown inmates. The typical criminal mentality sees imprisonment as a calculated risk for a particular criminal act. One's prison term is more or less rationally predictable. The function of racism in the judicial-penal complex is to shatter that predictability. The black burglar, anticipating a two- to four-year term, may end up doing ten to fifteen years, while the white burglar leaves after two years.

Within the contained, coercive universe of the prison, the captive is confronted with the realities of racism, not simply as individual acts dictated by attitudinal bias; rather he is compelled to come to grips with racism as an institutional phenomenon collectively experienced by the victims. The disproportionate representation of the black and brown communities, the manifest racism of parole boards, the intense brutality inherent in the relationship between prison guards and black and brown inmates—all this and more causes the prisoner to be confronted daily, hourly, with the concentrated, systematic existence of racism.

For the innocent prisoner, the process of radicalization should come easy; for the "guilty" victim, the insight into the nature of racism as it manifests itself in the judicial-penal complex can lead to a questioning of his own past criminal activity and a re-evaluation of the methods he has used to survive in a racist and exploitative society. Needless to say, this process is not automatic, it does not occur spontaneously. The persistent educational work carried out by the prison's political activists plays a key role in developing the political potential of captive men and women.

Prisoners—especially blacks, Chicanos, and Puerto Ricans—are increasingly advancing the proposition that they are *political* prisoners. They contend that they are political prisoners in the sense that they are largely the victims of an oppressive politico-economic order, swiftly becoming conscious of the causes underlying their victimization. . . .

Racist oppression invades the lives of black people on an infinite variety of levels. Blacks are imprisoned in a world where our labor and toil hardly allow us to eke out a decent existence, if we are able to find jobs at all. When the economy begins to falter, we are forever the first victims, always the most deeply wounded. When the economy is on its feet, we continue to live in a depressed state. Unemployment is generally twice as high in the ghettos as it is in the country as a whole and even higher among black women and youth. The unemployment rate among black youth has presently skyrocketed to 30 percent. If one-third of America's white youths were without a means of livelihood, we would either be in the thick of revolution or else under the iron rule of fascism. Substandard schools; medical care hardly fit for animals; overpriced, dilapidated housing; a welfare system based on a policy of skimpy concessions, designed to degrade and divide (and even this may soon be canceled)—this is only the beginning of the list of props in the overall scenery of oppression which, for the mass of blacks, is the universe.

In black communities, wherever they are located, there exists an ever-present reminder that our universe must remain stable in its drabness, its poverty, its brutality. From Birmingham to Harlem to Watts, black ghettos are occupied, patrolled and often attacked by massive deployments of police. The police, domestic caretakers of violence, are the oppressor's emissaries, charged with the task of containing us within the boundaries of our oppression. . . .

It goes without saying that the police would be unable to set into motion their racist machinery were they not sanctioned and supported by the judicial system. The courts not only consistently abstain from prosecuting criminal behavior on the part of the police, but they convict, on the basis of biased police testimony, countless black men and women. Court-appointed attorneys, acting in the twisted interests of overcrowded courts, convince 85 percent of the defendants to plead guilty. Even the manifestly innocent are advised to cop a plea so that the lengthy and expensive process of jury trials is avoided. This is the structure of the apparatus which summarily railroads black people into jails and prisons. (During my imprisonment in the New York Women's House of Detention, I encountered numerous cases involving innocent black women who had been advised to plead guilty. One sister had entered her white landlord's apartment for the purpose of paying rent. He attempted to rape her, and in the course of the ensuing struggle, a lit candle toppled over, burning a tablecloth. The landlord ordered her arrested for arson. Following the advice of her court-appointed attorney, she entered a guilty plea, having been deceived by the attorney's insistence that the court would be more lenient. The sister was sentenced to three years.)

The vicious circle linking poverty, police courts, and prison is an integral element of ghetto existence. Unlike the mass of whites, the path which leads to jails and prisons is deeply rooted in the imposed patterns of black existence. For this very reason, an almost instinctive affinity binds the mass of black people to the political prisoners. The vast majority of blacks harbor a deep hatred of the police and are not deluded by official proclamations of justice through the courts. . . .

Black people are rushing full speed ahead towards an understanding of the circumstances that give rise to exaggerated forms of political repression and thus an overabundance of political prisoners. This understanding is being forged out of the raw material of their own immediate experiences with racism. Hence, the black masses are growing conscious of their responsibility to defend those who are being persecuted for attempting to bring about the alleviation of the most injurious immediate problems facing black communities and ultimately to bring about total liberation through armed revolution, if it must come to this.

The black liberation movement is presently at a critical juncture. Fascist methods of repression threaten to physically decapitate and obliterate the movement. More subtle, yet no less dangerous, ideological tendencies from within threaten to isolate the black movement and diminish its revolutionary impact. Both menaces must be counteracted in order to ensure our survival. Revolutionary blacks must spearhead and provide leadership for a broad antifascist movement.

Fascism is a process, its growth and development are cancerous in nature. While today, the threat of fascism may be primarily restricted to the use of the law-enforcement–judicial-penal apparatus to arrest the overt and latent revolutionary trends among nationally oppressed people, tomorrow it may attack the working class *en masse* and eventually even moderate democrats. Even in this period, however, the cancer has already commenced to spread. In addition to the prison army of thousands and thousands of nameless Third World victims of political revenge, there are increasing numbers of white political prisoners—draft resisters, anti-war activists such as the Harrisburg Eight, men and women who have involved themselves on all levels of revolutionary activity.

Among the further symptoms of the fascist threat are official efforts to curtail the power of organized labor, such as the attack on the manifestly conservative construction workers and the trends to-wards reduced welfare aid. . . .

One of the fundamental historical lessons to be learned from past failures to prevent the rise of fascism is the decisive and indispens-able character of the fight against fascism in its incipient phases. Once allowed to conquer ground, its growth is facilitated in geomet-ric proportion. Although the most unbridled expressions of the fas-cist menace are still tied to the racist domination of blacks, Chicanos, Puerto Ricans, Indians, it lurks under the surface wherever there is potential resistance to the power of monopoly capital, the parasitic interests which control this society. Potentially it can profoundly worsen the conditions of existence for the average American citizen. Consequently, the masses of people in this country have a real, di-rect, and material stake in the struggle to free political prisoners, the struggle to abolish the prison system in its present form, the struggle against all dimensions of racism.

No one should fail to take heed of Georgi Dimitrov's warning: "Whoever does not fight the growth of fascism at these preparatory stages is not in a position to prevent the victory of fascism, but, on the contrary, facilitates that victory" (Report to the VIIth Congress of the Communist International, 1935). The only effective guarantee against the victory of fascism is an indivisible mass movement which refuses to conduct business as usual as long as repression rages on. It is only natural that blacks and other Third World peoples must lead this movement, for we are the first and most deeply injured victims of fascism. But it must embrace all potential victims and, most impor-tant, all working-class people, for the key to the triumph of fascism is its ideological victory over the entire working class. Given the erup-tion of a severe economic crisis, the door to such an ideological vic-tory can be opened by the active approval or passive toleration of racism. It is essential that white workers become conscious that, his-torically, through their acquiescence in the capitalist-inspired oppres-sion of blacks, they have only rendered themselves more vulnerable to attack.

The pivotal struggle which must be waged in the ranks of the working class is consequently the open, unreserved battle against entrenched racism. The white worker must become conscious of the threads which bind him to a James Johnson, a black auto worker, member of UAW, and a political prisoner presently facing charges for the killings of two foremen and a job setter. The merciless proliferation of the power of monopoly capital may ultimately push him inexorably down the very same path of desperation. No potential victim [of the fascist terror] should be without the knowledge that the greatest menace to racism and fascism is unity!

MARIN COUNTY JAIL
May, 1971

25. AMERICAN INDIAN MOVEMENT

Trail of Broken Treaties
(1972)

Founded in the summer of 1968 by Native American activists in Minneapolis, Minnesota, **THE AMERICAN INDIAN MOVEMENT (AIM)** embodied the radical spirit of the 1960s and 1970s. Specifically, AIM advocated a more militant protest strategy toward ongoing federal discrimination against Indian tribes throughout the United States. Positioning themselves as "outsiders," their approach reflected a growing frustration with the broken promises of the American government, as well as those who sought to reform the system from within. AIM continues to exist, but its political heyday came in the early 1970s. In November 1972, activists organized the Trail of Broken Treaties march from Minneapolis to Washington, D.C., where they occupied the federal headquarters of the Bureau of Indian Affairs. The following spring, AIM members seized the Pine Ridge Reservation in South Dakota—site of the infamous Wounded Knee massacre in 1873—which led to a violent seventy-one-day standoff with federal troops and agents. The "Trail of Broken Treaties" was AIM's twenty-point manifesto, a clarion call for political self-determination and cultural renewal. It was also a bold articulation of collective grievances accumulated through centuries of displacement, destruction, and disfranchisement.

SOURCE: http://www.aimovement.org/ggc/trailofbrokentreaties.html

SELECTED READINGS: Dennis Banks and Richard Erdoes, *Ojibwa Warrior: Dennis Banks and the Rise of the American Indian Movement* (2004); Paul Chaat Smith and Robert Allen Warrior, *Like a Hurricane: The Indian Movement from Alcatraz to Wounded Knee* (1997); Mary Crow Dog and Richard Erdoes, *Lakota Woman* (1990); and Kenneth S. Stern, *Loud Hawk: The United States Versus the American Indian Movement* (1994).

1. Restoration of Constitutional Treaty-Making Authority:

The U.S. President should propose by executive message, and the Congress should consider and enact legislation, to repeal the provision in the 1871 Indian Appropriations Act which withdrew federal recognition from Indian Tribes and Nations as political entities, which could be contracted by treaties with the United States, in order that the President may resume the exercise of his full constitutional authority for acting in the matters of Indian Affairs—and in order that Indian Nations may represent their own interests in the manner and method envisioned and provided in the Federal Constitution.

2. Establishment of Treaty Commission to Make New Treaties:

The President should impanel and the Congress establish, with next year, a Treaty Commission to contract a security and assistance treaty of treaties, with Indian people to negotiate a national commitment to the future of Indian people for the last quarter of the Twentieth Century. Authority should be granted to allow tribes to contract by separate and individual treaty, [and] multi-tribal or regional groupings or national collective, respecting general or limited subject matter . . . and provide that no provisions of existing treaty agreements may be withdrawn or in any manner affected without the explicit consent and agreement of any particularly related Indian Nation.

3. An Address to the American People
& Joint Sessions of Congress:

The President and the leadership of Congress should make a commitment now and next January to request and arrange for four Native Americans—selected by Indian people at a future date—and the President of the United States and any designated U.S. Senators and Representatives to address a joint session of Congress and the American people through national communications media regarding the Indian future within the American Nation, and relationships between the Federal Government and Indian Nations—on or before June 2, 1974, the first half-century anniversary of the 1924 "Indian Citizenship Act."

4. Commission to Review Treaty
Commitments & Violations:

The President should immediately create a multi-lateral Indian and non-Indian Commission to review domestic treaty commitments and complaints of chronic violations and to recommend or act for corrective actions, including the imposition of mandatory sanctions or interim restraints upon violative activities, and including formulation of legislation designed to protect the jeopardized Indian rights and eliminate the unending patterns of prohibitively complex lawsuits and legal defenses—which habitually have produced indecisive and indeterminate results, only too frequently forming guidelines for more court battles, or additional challenges and attacks against Indian rights. (Indians have paid attorneys and lawyers more than $40,000,000 since 1962. Yet many Indian people are virtually imprisoned in the nation's courtrooms, being forced constantly to defend their rights, [and] many tribes are forced to maintain a multitude of suits in numerous jurisdictions relating to the same or a single issue, or a few similar issues. There is less need for more attorney assurances than there is for institution of protections that reduce violations and minimize the possibilities for attacks upon Indian rights).

5. Resubmission of Unratified Treaties to the Senate:

The President should resubmit to the U.S. Senate of the next Congress those treaties negotiated with Indian nations or their representatives, but never heretofore ratified or rendered moot by subsequent treaty contract with such Indians not having ratified treaties with the United States. The primary purpose to be served shall be that of restoring the rule of law to the relationships between such Indians and the United States, and resuming a recognition of rights controlled by treaty relations where the failure to ratify prior treaties operated to affirm the cessions and loss of title to Indian lands and territory but failed to secure and protect the reservations of lands, rights, and resources reserved against cession, relinquishment, or loss. The Senate should adopt resolutions certifying that a prior de facto ratification has been affected by the Government of the United States, and direct that appropriate actions be undertaken to restore to such Indians an equitable measure of their reserved rights and ownership in lands, resources, and rights of self-government. Additionally, the President and the Congress should direct that reports be concluded upon the disposition of land rights and land title which were lawfully vested or held, for people of Native Indian blood, under the 1840 Treaty of Guadalupe Hidalgo with Mexico.

6. All Indians to Be Governed by Treaty Relations:

The Congress should enact a Joint Resolution declaring that, as a matter of public policy and good faith, all Indian people in the United States shall be considered to be in treaty relations with the Federal Government and governed by doctrines of such relationship.

7. Mandatory Relief Against Treaty Rights Violations:

The Congress should add a new section to Title 28 of the United States Code to provide for the judicial enforcement and protection of

Indian Treaty Rights. Such a section should direct that upon petition of any Indian Tribe or prescribed Indian groups and individuals claiming substantial injury, or interference in the equitable and good faith exercise of any rights, governing authority or utilization and preservation of resources secured by Treaty, mandatorily the Federal District courts shall grant immediate enjoinder or injunctive relief against any non-Indian party or defendants, including State governments and their subdivisions or officers alleged to be engaged in such injurious actions, until such time as the U.S. District Court may be reasonably satisfied that a Treaty Violation is not being committed or . . . that the Indians' interests and rights, in equity and in law, are preserved and protected from jeopardy and secure from harm.

8. Judicial Recognition of Indian Right to Interpret Treaties:

The Congress should by law provide for a new system of federal court jurisdiction and procedure, when Indian treaty or governmental rights are at issue, and when there are non-Indian parties involved in the controversy, whereby an Indian Tribe or Indian party may by motion advance the case from a federal District Court for hearing, and decision by the related U.S. Circuit Court of Appeals. The law should provide that, once an Interpretation upon the matter has been rendered by either a federal district or circuit court, an Indian Nation may, on its own behalf or on behalf of any of its members, if dissatisfied with the federal court ruling or regarding it in error respecting treaty or tribal rights, certify directly to the United States Supreme Court a "Declaratory Judgment of Interpretation" regarding the contested rights, . . . drawn at the direction or under the auspices of the affected Indian Nation, which that Court shall be mandated to receive with the contested decision for hearing and final judgment and resolution of the controversy—except and unless that any new treaties which might be contracted may provide for some other impartial body for making ultimate and final interpretations of treaty provisions and their application. In addition, the law should provide

that an Indian Nation, to protect its exercise of rights or the exercise
of treaty or tribal rights by its members, or when engaging in new
activities based upon sovereign or treaty rights, may issue an interim "Declaratory Opinion on Interpretation of Rights," which
shall be controlling upon the exercise of police powers or administrative authorities of that Indian Nation, the United States or any
State(s), unless or until successfully challenged or modified upon
certification to and decision by the United States Supreme Court—
and not withstanding any contrary U.S. Attorney General's
opinion(s) . . . solicitor's opinion(s), or Attorney General's Opinion(s)
of any of the States.

9. Creation of Congressional Joint Committee
on Reconstruction of Indian Relations:

The next Congress of the United States, and its respective houses,
should agree at its outset and in its organization to withdraw jurisdiction over Indian Affairs and Indian-related program authorizations from all existing Committees except Appropriations of the
House and Senate, and create a Joint House-Senate "Committee on
Reconstruction of Indian Relations and Programs" to assume such
jurisdiction and responsibilities for recommending new legislation
and program authorizations to both houses of Congress—including
consideration and action upon all proposals presented herewith by
the "Trail of Broken Treaties Caravan," as well as matters from
other sources. The Joint Committee membership should consist of
Senators and Representatives who would be willing to commit considerable amounts of time and labor and conscientious thought to
an exhaustive review and . . . evaluation of past and present policies, programs and practices of the Federal Government relating to
Indian people, to the development of a comprehensive, broadly in-
clusive "American Indian Community Reconstruction Act," which
shall provide for certain of the measures herein proposed, repeal
numerous laws which have oppressively disallowed the existence
of a viable "Indian Life" in this country, and . . . construct the pro-

visions which shall allow and ensure a secure Indian future in America.

10. Land Reform and Restoration of a 110-Million-Acre Native Land Base:

The next Congress and Administration should commit themselves and effect a national commitment implemented by statutes or executive and administrative actions to restore a permanent non-diminishing Native American land base of not less than 110 million acres by July 4, 1976. This land base and its separate parts should be vested with the recognized rights and conditions of being perpetually non-taxable except by autonomous and sovereign Indian authority, and should never again be permitted to be alienated from Native American or Indian ownership and control.

A. Priorities in Restoration of the Native American Land Base

When Congress acted to delimit the President's authority and the Indian Nations' powers for making treaties in 1871, approximately 135,000,000 acres of land and territory had been secured to Indian ownership against cession or relinquishment. This acreage did not include the 1867 treaty-secured recognition of land title and rights of Alaskan Natives, nor millions of acres otherwise retained by Indians in what were to become "unrelated" treaties of Indian land cession, as in California; nor other land areas authorized to be set aside for Indian Nations contracted by, but never benefiting from, their treaties. When the Congress, in 1887, under the General Allotment Act and other measures of the period and "single system of legislation," delegated treaty-assigned Presidential responsibilities to the Secretary of the Interior and his Commissioner of Indian Affairs and agents in the Bureau of Indian Affairs, relating to the government of Indian relations under the treaties for the 135 million acres, [the land,] collectively held, immediately became subject to loss. The 1887 Act provided for the sale of "surplus" Indian lands—and contained a formula for the assignment or allocation of land tracts to Indian individuals, dependent partly on family size, which would have allowed an average-sized allotment of 135 acres to one million Indians—at a time when the number of tribally related Indians was less than a quarter million or fewer than 200,000. The Interior Department efficiently managed the loss of 100 million acres of Indian land and its transfer to non-Indian ownership (frequently by homestead, not direct purchase) in little more then the next quarter century. When Congress prohibited further allotments to Indian individuals, by its 1934 Indian Reorganization Act, it effectively determined that future generations of Indian people would be "landless Indians" except by hiership and inheritance. 110 million acres, including 40 million acres in Alaska, would approximate an average 135 acres multiplied by .8 million Native Americans, a number indicated by the 1970 U.S. Census. Simple justice would seem to demand that priorities in restorations of land bases be granted to those Indian Nations who are land-less by fault of unratified or unfulfilled treaty provisions Indian Nations [who are] land-less because of congressional and administrative actions reflective of criminal abuse of trust responsibilities; and other groupings of land-less Indians, particularly of the land-less generations, including many urban Indians and non-reservation Indian people, many of whom have been forced to pay in forms of deprivation, loss of rights and entitlements, and other extreme costs upon their lives an "emigration-migration-education-training" tax for their unfulfilled pursuit of opportunity in America—a "tax" as unwarranted and unjustified as it is unprecedented in the history of human rights–mature nations possessed of a modern conscience.

B. Consolidation of Indians' Land, Water, [and] Natural and Economic Resources:

The restoration of an equitable Native American Land Base should be accompanied by enlightened revision in the present character of alleged "trust relationships" and by reaffirmation of the creative and positive characters of Indian sovereignty and sovereign rights. The past pattern of treating "trust status" as wrongful "non-ownership" of properties beyond control of individual interests and "owners" could be converted to a beneficial method of consolidating useable land, water, forests, fisheries, and other exploitable and renewable natural resources into productive economic, cultural, or other community-purpose units, benefiting both individual and tribal interests in direct forms under autonomous control of properly defined, appropriate levels of Indian government. For example, the 135 million acres of multiple and fractionated hiership lands should not represent a collective denial of beneficial ownership and interests of inheriting individuals, but [should rather] be considered for plans of collective and consolidated use. (The alternatives and complexities of this subject and its discussion require the issuance of a separate essay at a later date.)

C. Termination of Losses and Condemnation of Non-Indian Land Title:

Most short-term and long-term leases of some four million acres of Indians' agricultural and industrial-use lands represent a constant pattern of mismanagement of trust responsibilities, with the federal trustees knowingly and willfully administering properties in methods and terms which are adverse or inimical to the interests of the Indian beneficiaries and their tribes. Non-Indians have benefit of the best of Indian agricultural range and dry farm lands, and of some irrigation systems, generally having the lowest investment/highest return ratios, while Indians are relegated to lands requiring high investments/low returns. A large-scale, if selective, program of lease cancellations and non-renewals should be instituted under Congressional authorization as quickly as possible. As well, Indian Tribes should be authorized to re-secure Indian ownership of alienated lands within reservation boundaries under a system of condemnation for national policy purposes, with the federal government bearing the basic costs of "just compensation" as burden for unjustified betrayals of its trust responsibilities to Indian people. These actions would [in] no way be as extreme as the termination, nationalization, confiscation and sale of millions of acres of reservation land by a single measure, as in the cases of the Menominee and Klamath Indian Tribes, and attempted repeatedly with the Colvilles.

D. Repeal of the Menominee, Klamath, and Other Termination Acts:

The Congress should act immediately to repeal the Termination Acts of the 1950s and 1960s and restore ownership of the several

million acres of land to the Indian people involved, [to be] perpetually non-alienable and tax-exempt. The Indians' rights to autonomous self-government and sovereign control of their resources and
development should be reinstated. Repeal of the terminal legislation
would also advance a commitment towards a collective 110-million-acre
land base for Native Americans—when added to the near 55 million
acres already held by Indians, apart from the additional 40 million
acres allocated in Alaska. (The impact of termination and its various
forms have never been understood fully by the American people, the
Congress, and many Indian people. Few wars between nations have
ever accomplished as much as the total dispossession of a people of
their rights and resources as have the total victories and total surren-
ders legislated by the Termination Laws. If the Arab States of the
present Mid-East could comparably presume the same authority over
the State of Israel, they could eliminate Israel by purchase or by declaring it an Arab State or subdivision thereof; on the one hand,
evicting the Israelis from the newly acquired Arab lands, or, on the
other, allowing the Israelis to remain as part of the larger Arab Nation and justify the disposition to the world by the claim that,
whether leaving or remaining, but without their nation, the Jewish
people would still be Jewish. Such an unacceptable outrage to American people would quickly succeed to World War III—except when
such actions are factually taken against Menominees, Klamaths,
Senecas, [and] Utes, and threatened against many other landed nations of Indian people.

11. Revision Of 25 U.S.C. 163; Restoration of Rights to Indians Terminated by Enrollment and Revocation of Prohibitions Against "Dual Benefits":

The Congress should enact measures fully in support of the doctrine
that an Indian Nation has complete power to govern and control its
own membership, eradicating the extortive and coercive devices in
federal policy and programming which have subverted and denied

the natural human relationships and natural development of Indian communities and committed countless injuries upon Indian families and individuals. The general prohibition against benefiting dually from federal assistance or tribal resources by having membership or maintaining relationships in more than one Indian Tribe has frequently resulted in denial of rights and benefits from many sources. Blood quantum criteria, closed and restrictive enrollment, and "dual benefits prohibitions" have generated minimal problems for Indians having successive non-Indian parentage involved in their ancestry— while creating vast problems and complexities for full-blood and predominant–Indian blood persons, when ancestry or current relationships involve two separate Indian tribes or more. Full-blood Indians can fail to qualify for membership in any of several tribes to which they may be directly related if quantum relationships happen to be in wrong configuration, or non-qualifying factions. Families have been divided to be partly included upon enrollments, while some children of the same parents are wrongly (if there are at all to be enrollments) excluded. There should be a restoration of Indian and tribal rights to all individual Indians who have been victimized and deprived by the vicious forms of termination effected by forced choices between multiply related Tribes, abusive application of blood-quantum criteria, and federally engineered and federally approved enrollments. The right of Indian persons to maintain, sever, or resume valid relations with several Indian Nations or communities unto which they are born, or acquire relationships through natural marriage relations or parenthood and other customary forms, must again be recognized under law and practice, [as well as] the right of Indian Nations to receive other Indian people into relations with them—or to maintain relations with all their own people, without regard to blood-quantum criteria and federal standards for exclusion or restrictions upon benefits. (It may be recognized that the general Indian leadership has become conditioned to accept and give application to these forms of terminating rights, patterns which are an atrocious aberration from any concepts of Indian justice and sovereignty).

12. Repeal of State Laws Enacted
Under Public Law 280 (1953):

State enactments under the authority conferred by the Congress in Public Law 280 has posed the most serious threat to Indian sovereignty and local self-government of any measure in recent decades. Congress must now nullify those State statutes. Represented as a "law enforcement" measure, PL280 robs Indian communities of the core of their governing authority and operates to convert reservation areas into refuges from responsibilities, where many people, not restricted by race, can take full advantage of a veritable vacuum of controlling law, or law which commands its first respect for justice by encouraging an absence of offenses. These States' acceptance of condition for their own statehood in their Enabling Acts—that they forever disclaim sovereignty and jurisdiction over Indian lands and Indian people—should be binding upon them and restrictive condition upon their sovereignty be reinstated. They should not be permitted further to gain from the conflict of interest engaged by such States' participation in enactment of Public Law 280 at the expense of the future of Indian people in their own communities, as well as our present welfare and well-being.

13. Resume Federal Protective Jurisdiction
for Offenses Against Indians:

The Congress should enact, the Administration support and seek passage of, new provisions under Titles 18 and 25 of the U.S. Code [to] . . . extend the protective jurisdiction of the United States over Indian persons wherever situated in its territory and the territory of the several States outside of Indian Reservations or Country and provide [that] prescribed offenses of violence against Indian persons shall be federal crimes, punishable by prescribed penalties through prosecutions in the federal judiciary, and enforced in arrest actions by the Federal Bureau of Investigation. U.S. Marshals and other commissioned police agents of the United States . . . shall be compelled to act upon the commission of such crimes and upon any written complaint or sworn request alleging an offense, which by itself would be deemed probable cause for arresting actions.

A. Establishment of a National Federal Indian Grand Jury:

The Congress should establish a special national grand jury consisting solely of Indian members selected in part by the President and in part by Indian people, having a continuous life, and equipped with its own investigative and legal staff, and presided over by competent judicial officers, while vested with prescribed authorities of indictments to be prosecuted in the federal and Indian court systems. This grand jury should be granted jurisdiction to act in the bringing of indictments on basis of evidence and probable cause within any federal judicial district where a crime of violence has been committed against an Indian and resulting [either] in an Indian's death or in bodily injury and involving lethal weapons or aggressive force, when finding reason to be not satisfied with handling or disposition of a case or incident by local authorities, and operating consistent with federal constitutional standards respecting [the] rights of [the] accused. More broadly and generally, the grand jury should be granted broad authority to monitor the enforcement of law under Titles 18, 25, and 42 respecting Indian jurisdiction and civil rights protections; the administration of law enforcement; confinement facilities and juvenile detention centers, and judicial systems in Indian country; corrupt practices or violations of law in the administration of federal Indian agencies or of federally funded programs for Indian people—including administration by tribal officials or tribal governmental units—and federal employees; and issue special reports bringing indictments when warranted, directed toward elimination of wrong-doing, wrongful administration or practices, and improvement recommendations for systems to ensure proper services and benefits to communities, or Indian people.

B. Jurisdiction over Non-Indians Within Indian Reservations:

The Congress should eliminate the immunity of non-Indians to the general application of law and law enforcement within Reservation

Boundaries, without regard to land or property title. Title 18 of the U.S. Code should be amended to clarify and compel that all persons within the originally established boundaries of an Indian Reservation are subject to the laws of the sovereign Indian Nation in the exercise of its autonomous governing authority. A system of concurrent jurisdiction should be minimum requirement in incorporated towns.

C. Accelerated Rehabilitation and Release Program for State and Federal Indian Prisoners:

The Administration should immediately contract an appropriately staffed Commission of Review on Rehabilitation of Indian Prisoners in Federal and State institutions, funded from Safe Streets and Crime Control funds or discretionary funds under control of the President, and consisting of Indian membership. The review commission would conduct a census and survey of all Indian prisoners presently confined and compile information on records of offenses, sentences, actions of committing jurisdictions (courts, police, pre-sentence reports, probation and parole systems) and related pertinent data. The basic objective of the review commission would be to arrange for the development of new systems of community treatment centers or national/regional rehabilitation centers as alternatives to existing prison situations, to work with Bureau of Prison and federal parole systems to arrange for accelerated rehabilitation and release programs as justified, and to give major attention to the reduction of offenses and recidivism in Indian communities. The commission would act to provide forms by which Indian people may assume the largest measures of responsibility in reversing the rapidly increasing crime rates on Indian reservations and re-approach situations where needs for jails and prisoner institutions may again be virtually eliminated. The Congress should provide appropriate authorizations in support of such effort—perhaps extending the protective jurisdiction of the United States over Indians in state institutions to provide for transfer to Indian-operated rehabilitation and treatment centers, at least probation systems, in a bargain of responsibility for bringing about vast reduction in incidences of offenses among Indian communities. (The

$8,000,000 BIA budget for Law and Order is not directed toward such purpose—spending nearly half of its present increases on new cars to gauge the increases in reported offenses.)

Note on 13-13c

The U.S. has asserted its jurisdiction over Indians nationwide, and may now do so again protectively. The Congress controlled liquor sales to Indians nationally until 1953, allowing prosecution for non-Indian offenders. Education of Indians in public state schools is essentially a contracting of jurisdiction to States.)

14. Abolition of the Bureau of Indian Affairs by 1976:

. . . The Congress working through the proposed Senate-House "Joint Committee on Reconstruction of Indian Relations and Programs," in formulation of an Indian Community Reconstruction Act, should direct that the Bureau of Indian Affairs shall be abolished as an agency on or before July 4, 1976, to provide for an alternative structure of government for sustaining and revitalizing the Indian-federal relationship between the President and the Congress of the United States, respectively, and the Indian Nations and Indian people at last consistent with constitutional criteria, national treaty commitments, and Indian sovereignty, and [to] provide for transformation and transition into the new system as rapidly as possible prior to abolition of the BIA.

15. Creation of an Office of Federal Indian Relations and Community Reconstruction:

The Bureau of Indian Affairs should be replaced by a new unit in the federal government which represents an equality of responsibility among and between the President, the Congress, and the Governments of the separate Indian Nations (or their respective people collectively), and [grants] equal standing in the control of relations between the Federal Government and Indian Nations. The following standards and conditions should be obtained:

A. The Office would structurally be placed in the Executive Offices of the President, but [would] be directed by a tripartite Commission of three Commissioners, one being appointed by the President, one being appointed by the joint congressional committee, and one being selected by national election among Indian people, and all three requiring confirmation by the U.S. Senate.

B. The Office would be directly responsible to the President, the Congress, and [the] Indian people, represented by a newly-established National Indian Council of no more than twenty members selected by combination [of] national and regional elections for two-year terms with half expiring each year.

C. All existing federal agencies and program units presently involved or primarily directed toward serving Indians would be consolidated under the office, together with the budget allocations of the Departments assisting Indians, although primarily oriented toward other concerns. All programs would be reviewed for revision of form, elimination altogether, or continuance.

D. A total personnel and employee structure ceiling of no more than 1,000 employees in all categories should be placed upon the new office for its first five years of operation. Employment in the new office would be exempt from Civil Service regulations and provisions. (The Civil Service Commission and federal employee unions should be requested to propose a plan for preference hiring in other agencies and for transfer of benefits to new employment, for presentation to Congress, incident to abolition of the BIA and other Indian-related federal programs.)

E. The Office would maintain responsibility over its own budget and planning functions, independent from any control by the Office of Management and Budget (OMB), and should be authorized

$15,000,000,000 budget, reviewing the efficiency of the Office and the impact and progress of the programming. The Appropriations Committees should not impose undue interference in plans, but should insist upon equitable treatment of all Indian Nations and general Indian people who would not be denied their respective direct relations with the Congress or with the President.

F. The Office of Federal Indian Relations would assume the administrative responsibility as trustee of Indian properties and property rights until revision of the trust responsibility might be accomplished and delegated for administration as a function and expression of the sovereign authority of the respective Indian Nations.

16. Priorities and Purpose of the Proposed New Office:

The central purpose of the proposed "Office of Federal Indian Relations and Community Reconstruction" is to remedy the break-down in constitutionally prescribed relationships between the United States and Indian Nations and people and to alleviate the destructive impact that [the] distortion in those relationships has rendered upon the lives of Indian people. More directly, it is proposed for allowing broad attacks upon the multitude of millions of problems which confront Indian lives, or consume them, and which cannot be eliminated by piecemeal approaches, jerry-built structures, bureaucracies, or by taking on one problem at a time, always to be confronted by many more. The Congress, with assent of the Courts, has developed its constitutional mandate to "regulate Indian commerce" into a doctrine of absolute control and total power over the lives of Indians—through failing to give these concerns the time and attention that the responsibilities of such power demand. The Congress restricted the highest authority of the President for dealing with Indian matters and affairs, then abandoned Indian people to the lowest levels of bureaucratic government for administration of its part-time care, [where it] asserted all-powerful control. The constitution maintained Indian people in citizenship and allegiance to our own Nations, but the

Congress and the Bureau of Indian Affairs has converted this constitutional standard into the most bastardized forms of acknowledged
autonomy and "sovereign self-governing control"—scarcely worthy
of the terms, if remaining divested of their meaning. A central priority of the proposed Office should be the formulation of legislation
designed to repeal the body of Indian Law that continues to operate
most harmfully against Indian communities—including sections of
the 1934 Indian Reorganization Act and prior legislation which instituted foreign forms of government upon our Nations, or which
have served to divorce tribal government from responsibilities and
accountability to Indian people. At this point in time, there is demonstrable need for the Congress to exercise highest responsibilities
to Indian people in order that we might have a future in our homeland. This requires that Congress now recognize some restrictions
upon its own authority to intervene in Indian communities and act
to totally exclude the exercise of local tribal sovereignty and self-
governing control. The proposed Office of Federal Indian Relations
and Community Reconstruction should be authorized the greatest
latitude to act and to remove restrictions from the positive actions of
Indian people. This can be achieved if the Congress establishes a
new Office in the manner proposed and authorizes it in promising
degree to operate as [an instrument] of its responsibilities.

17. Indian Commerce and Tax Immunities:

The Congress should enact a statute or Joint Resolution certifying
that trade, commerce, and transportation of Indians remain wholly
outside the authority, control, and regulation of the several States.
Congressional acts should provide that complete taxing authority
upon properties, use of properties and incomes derived therefrom,
and business activities within the exterior boundaries of Indian reservations, as well as commerce between reservations and Indian
Nations, shall be vested with the respective or related tribal governments, or their appropriate to subdivisions—or certify that consistent

with the Fourteenth Amendment, Section 2 statehood enabling acts, prevailing treaty commitments, and the general policy of the United States, that total Indian immunity to taxing authority of states is re-affirmed and extended with uniformity to all Indian Nations as a matter of established or vested right. (These questions should not have to be constantly carried to the courts for reaffirmation—disregarded as general law and attacked by challenge with every discernable variation or difference in fact not considered at a prior trial, Tribes have been restricted in their taxing authorities by some of the same laws which exclude federal or state authority. However, there are areas where taxing authorities might be used beneficially in the generation of revenues for financing government functions, services, and community institutions.) (The Congress should remove any obstacles to the rights of Indian people to travel freely between Indian Nations without being blocked in movement, commerce, or trade, by barriers of borders, customs, duties, or tax.)

18. Protection of Indians' Religious Freedom and Cultural Integrity:

The Congress shall proclaim its insistence that the religious freedom and cultural integrity of Indian people shall be respected and protected throughout the United States, and provide that Indian religion and culture, even in regenerating or renaissance or developing stages, or when manifested in the personal character and treatment of one's own body, shall not be interfered with, disrespected, or denied. (No Indian shall be forced to cut their hair by any institution or public agency or official, including military authorities or prison regulation, for example.) It should be an insistence by Congress that implies strict penalty for its violation.

19. National Referendums, Local Options, and Forms of Indian Organization:

The Indian population is small enough to be amenable to voting and elective processes of national referendums, local option referendums, and other elections for rendering decisions [and] approval or disapproval on many issues and matters. The steady proliferation of Indian and Indian-interest organizations, Indian advisory boards, and the like; the multiplication of Indian officials; and the emergence of countless Indian "leaders" represent a less preferable form for decision-making, a state of disorganization, and a clear reflection of deterioration in the relations between the United States and Indian people as contracting sovereigns holding a high standard of accountability and responsibility. Some Indians seem to stand by to ratify any viewpoints relating to any or all Indians; others [are] conditioned to accept any viewpoint or proposal from [an] official source. Whereas Indian people were to be secure from political manipulation and the general political system in the service of Indian needs, political favor and cutthroat competition for funds with grants made among limited alliances of agency, Indian friends have become the rule—while responsibilities and accountability to Indian people and Indian communities have been forgotten. While the treaty relationship allows that we should not be deprived by power what we are possessed of by right, little personal power and political games are being played by a few Indians while we are being deprived our rights. This dissipation of strength, energies, and commitment should end. We should consolidate our resources and purpose to restore relations born of sovereignty and to resume command of our communities, our rights, our resources, and our destiny. (The National Council on Indian Opportunity, Association on American Indian Affairs, and the National Tribal Chairman's Association are examples of government, non-Indian directed, and Indian organizations which are among many which could and should be eliminated. At least none should be funded from federal sources).

20. Health, Housing, Employment, Economic Development, and Education:

The Congress and Administration and proposed Indian Community Reconstruction Office must allow for the most creative, if demanding and disciplined, forms of community development and purposeful initiatives. The proposed $15,000,000,000 budget for the 1970s remainder could provide for completed construction of 100,000 new housing units; create more than 100,000 new permanent, income- and tribal revenue–producing jobs on reservations; and lay foundation for as many more in years following; meet all the economic and industrial development needs of numerous communities; and make education at all levels, [as well as] health services or medical care, [available] to all Indians a matter of entitlement and fulfilled right. Yet, we now find most Indians unserved and programs not keeping pace with growing problems under a billion-dollar-plus budget annually—approximately a service cost of $10,000 per reservation Indian family per year, or $100,000 in this decade. Our fight is not over a $50-million cutback in a mismanaged and misdirected budget, and cannot be ended with restoration of that then-invisible amount, but over the part that it, any and all amounts, have come to play in a perennial billion-dollar indignity upon the lives of Indian people, our aged, our young, our parents, and our children. Death remains a standard cure for environmentally induced diseases afflicting many Indian children without adequate housing facilities, heating systems, and pure water sources. Their delicate bodies provide their only defense and protection—and too often their own body processes become allies to the quickening of their deaths, as with numerous cases of dysentery and diarrhea. Still more has been spent on hotel bills for Indian-related problem-solving meetings, conferences, and conventions than has been spent on needed housing in recent years. More is being spent from federal and tribal fund sources on such decision-making activities than is being committed to assist but two-thirds of Indian college students having desperate financial need. Rather, few decisions are made, and less problems solved, because there has developed an insensitivity to conscience which has eliminated basic standards of accountability. Indian communities have been fragmented in governmental, social, and constitutional functions as they have become restructured or de-structured to accommodate the fragmentation in governmental programming and contradictions in federal policies. There is a need to reintegrate these functions into the life and fabric of the communities. Of treaty provisions standard to most treaties, none has been breached more viciously and often as those dealing with education—first by withdrawing education processes from jurisdiction and responsibility of Indian communities, and from the power of Indian self-government—and failing yet to restore authority to our people, except through increased funding of old advisory and contract-delegation laws, or through control to conduct school in the conditioned forms and systems devised by non-Indians, or otherwise commended by current popularity. At minimum, Indian Nations have to reclaim community education authority to allow creative education processes in forms of their free choice, in a system of federally sanctioned units or consolidated Indian districts, supported by a mandatory recognition of accreditation in all other systems in this land.

26. PETER SINGER

Animal Liberation
(1975)

PETER SINGER's *Animal Liberation* (1975) has been called "the Bible of the Animal Liberation movement," and even today it continues to serve as this movement's intellectual bedrock. Singer (1946–) was born in Melbourne, Australia, and was educated at the University of Melbourne and Oxford. He has taught at Oxford, New York University, and Princeton University. Singer's work focuses on ethical issues and has long been controversial. In *Animal Liberation*, Singer wrote about "speciesm," the practice whereby most humans "sacrifice the most important interests of members of other species in order to promote the most trivial interests of our own species." His work promoted vegetarianism and helped inspire a global movement against "factory farms," as well as against unnecessarily cruel laboratory animal experimentation and product-testing procedures. Reprinted below is the preface to *Animal Liberation*.

SOURCE: Peter Singer, *Animal Liberation*. New York: Avon Books, 1975.

SELECTED READINGS: Gary L. Francione, *Rain Without Thunder: The Ideology of the Animal Rights Movement* (1996). Dale Jamieson, ed., *Singer and His Critics* (1999). Tom Regan, *All That Dwell Therein: Animal Rights and Environmental Ethics* (1982).

A liberation movement demands an expansion of our moral horizons. Practices that were previously regarded as natural and inevitable come to be seen as the result of an unjustifiable prejudice. Who can say with any confidence that none of his or her attitudes and practices can legitimately be questioned? If we wish to avoid being numbered among the oppressors, we must be prepared to rethink all our attitudes to other groups, including the most fundamental of them. We need to consider our attitudes from the point of view of those who suffer by them, and by the practices that follow from them. If we can make this unaccustomed mental switch, we may discover a pattern in our attitudes and practices that operates so as consistently to benefit the same group—usually the group to which we ourselves belong—at the expense of another group. So we come to see that there is a case for a new liberation movement.

The aim of this book is to lead you to make this mental switch in your attitudes and practices toward a very large group of beings: members of species other than our own. I believe that our present attitudes to these beings are based on a long history of prejudice and arbitrary discrimination. I argue that there can be no reason—except the selfish desire to preserve the privileges of the exploiting group—for refusing to extend the basic principle of equality of consideration to members of other species. I ask you to recognize that your attitudes to members of other species are a form of prejudice no less objectionable than prejudice about a person's race or sex.

In comparison with other liberation movements, Animal Liberation has a lot of handicaps. First and most obvious is the fact that members of the exploited group cannot themselves make an organized protest against the treatment they receive (though they can and do protest to the best of their abilities individually). We have to speak up on behalf of those who cannot speak for themselves. You can appreciate how serious this handicap is by asking yourself how long blacks would have had to wait for equal rights if they had not been able to stand up for themselves and demand it. The less able a group is to stand up and organize against oppression, the more easily it is oppressed.

More significant still for the prospects of the Animal Liberation movement is the fact that almost all of the oppressing group are directly involved in, and see themselves as benefiting from, the oppression. There are few humans indeed who can view the oppression of animals with the detachment possessed, say, by Northern whites debating the institution of slavery in the Southern states of the Union. People who eat pieces of slaughtered nonhumans every day find it hard to believe that they are doing wrong; and they also find it hard to imagine what else they could eat. On this issue, anyone who eats meat is an interested party. They benefit—or at least they think they benefit—from the present disregard of the interests of nonhuman animals. This makes persuasion more difficult. How many Southern slaveholders were persuaded by the arguments used by the Northern abolitionists, and accepted by nearly all of us today? Some, but not many. I can and do ask you to put aside your interest in eating meat when considering the arguments of this book; but I know from my own experience that with the best will in the world this is not an easy thing to do. For behind the mere momentary desire to eat meat on a particular occasion lie many years of habitual meat-eating which have conditioned our attitudes to animals.

Habit. That is the final barrier that the Animal Liberation movement faces. Habits not only of diet but also of thought and language must be challenged and altered. Habits of thought lead us to brush aside descriptions of cruelty to animals as emotional, for "animal-lovers only"; or if not that, then anyway the problem is so trivial in comparison to the problems of human beings that no sensible person could give it time and attention. This too is a prejudice—for how can one know that a problem is trivial until one has taken the time to examine its extent? Although in order to allow a more thorough treatment this book deals with only two of the many areas in which humans cause other animals to suffer, I do not think anyone who reads it to the end will ever again think that the only problems that merit time and energy are problems concerning humans.

The habits of thought that lead us to disregard the interests of animals can be challenged, as they are challenged in the following pages.

This challenge has to be expressed in a language, which in this case happens to be English. The English language, like other languages, reflects the prejudices of its users. So authors who wish to challenge these prejudices are in a well-known type of bind: either they use language that reinforces the very prejudices they wish to challenge, or else they fail to communicate with their audience. This book has already been forced along the former of these paths. We commonly use the word "animal" to mean "animals other than human beings." This usage sets humans apart from other animals, implying that we are not ourselves animals—an implication that everyone who has had elementary lessons in biology knows to be false.

In the popular mind, the term "animal" lumps together beings as different as oysters and chimpanzees while placing a gulf between chimpanzees and humans, although our relationship to those apes is much closer than the oyster's. Since there exists no other short term for the nonhuman animals, I have, in the title of this book and else-where in these pages, had to use "animal" as if it did not include the human animal. This is a regrettable lapse from the standards of revo-lutionary purity, but it seems necessary for effective communication. Occasionally, however, to remind you that this is a matter of conve-nience only, I shall use longer, more accurate modes of referring to what was once called "the brute creation." In other cases, too, I have tried to avoid language which tends to degrade animals or disguise the nature of the food we eat.

The basic principles of Animal Liberation are very simple. I have tried to write a book that is clear and easy to understand, requiring no expertise of any kind. It is necessary, however, to begin with a discus-sion of the principles that underlie what I have to say. While there should be nothing here that is difficult, readers unused to this kind of discussion might find the first chapter rather abstract. Don't be put off. In the next chapters we get down to the little-known details of how our species oppresses others under our control. There is nothing ab-stract about this oppression, or about the chapters that describe it.

If the recommendations made in the following chapters are ac-cepted, millions of animals will be spared considerable pain. More-over, millions of humans will benefit too. As I write, people are starving to death in many parts of the world; and many more are in imminent danger of starvation. The United States government has said that because of poor harvests and diminished stocks of grain it can provide only limited—and inadequate—assistance; but the heavy emphasis in affluent nations on rearing animals for food wastes several times as much food as it produces. By ceasing to rear and kill animals for food, we can make so much extra food available for humans that, properly distributed, it would eliminate starvation and malnutrition from this planet. Animal Liberation is Human Liberation too.

27.

The Combahee River Collective Statement
(1977)

The **"Combahee River Collective Statement"** is an important articulation of black feminist theory and practice. (The Collective gained its name from a South Carolina river where abolitionist Harriet Tubman helped free 750 slaves during the Civil War.) It was formed in Boston in 1974 in an effort to raise the consciousness of African-American women, especially around such issues as sexual harassment, classism, and heterosexism. It lasted until 1980. Although the following manifesto represented the collective thinking of several leading black feminists, it was primarily written by Barbara Smith (1946–) a pioneering literary critic and editor. According to one historian, it was "crucial to building the [black feminist movement] in the 1970s," and it continues to carry currency among black feminists today.

SOURCE: *The Combahee River Collective Statement: Black Feminist Organizing in the Seventies and Eighties.* Foreword by Barbara Smith. Latham, NY: Kitchen Table: Women of Color Press, 1986.

SELECTED READINGS: bell hooks, *Feminist Theory from Margin to Center* (1984). Barbara Smith, ed., *Home Girls: A Black Feminist Anthology* (1983). Barbara Smith, *Toward a Black Feminist Criticism* (1977).

. . . What We Believe

Above all else, our politics initially sprang from the shared belief that black women are inherently valuable, that our liberation is a necessity not as an adjunct to somebody else's but because of our need as human persons for autonomy. This may seem so obvious as to sound simplistic, but it is apparent that no other ostensibly progressive movement has ever considered our specific oppression a priority or worked seriously for the ending of that oppression. Merely naming the pejorative stereotypes attributed to black women (e.g., mammy, matriarch, Sapphire, whore, bulldagger), let alone cataloguing the cruel, often murderous, treatment we receive, indicates how little value has been placed upon our lives during four centuries of bondage in the Western Hemisphere. We realize that the only people who care enough about us to work consistently for our liberation is us. Our politics evolve from a healthy love for ourselves, our sisters, and our community, which allows us to continue our struggle and work.

This focusing upon our own oppression is embodied in the concept of identity politics. We believe that the most profound and potentially the most radical politics come directly out of our own identity, as opposed to working to end somebody else's oppression. In the case of black women this is a particularly repugnant, dangerous, threatening, and therefore revolutionary concept because it is obvious from looking at all the political movements that have preceded us that anyone is more worthy of liberation than ourselves. We reject pedestals, queenhood, and walking ten paces behind. To be recognized as human, levelly human, is enough.

We believe that sexual politics under patriarchy is as pervasive in black women's lives as are the politics of class and race. We also often find it difficult to separate race from class from sex oppression because in our lives they are most often experienced simultaneously. We know that there is such a thing as racial-sexual oppression that is neither solely racial nor solely sexual, e.g., the history of rape of black women by white men as a weapon of political repression.

Although we are feminists and lesbians, we feel solidarity with progressive black men and do not advocate the fractionalization that white women who are separatists demand. Our situation as black people necessitates that we have solidarity around the fact of race, which white women of course do not need to have with white men, unless it is their negative solidarity as racial oppressors. We struggle together with black men against racism, while we also struggle with black men about sexism.

We realize that the liberation of all oppressed peoples necessitates the destruction of the political-economic systems of capitalism and imperialism as well as patriarchy. We are socialists because we believe the work must be organized for the collective benefit of those who do the work and create the products, and not for the profit of the bosses. Material resources must be equally distributed among those who create these resources. We are not convinced, however, that a socialist revolution that is not also a feminist and antiracist revolution will guarantee our liberation. We have arrived at the necessity for developing an understanding of class relationships that takes into account the specific class position of black women who are generally marginal in the labor force, while at this particular time some of us are temporarily viewed as doubly desirable tokens at white-collar and professional levels. We need to articulate the real class situation of persons who are not merely raceless, sexless workers, but for whom racial and sexual oppression are significant determinants in their working/economic lives. Although we are in essential agreement with Marx's theory as it applied to the very specific economic relationships he analyzed, we know that this analysis must be extended further in order for us to understand our specific economic situation as black women.

A political contribution that we feel we have already made is the expansion of the feminist principle that the personal is political. In our consciousness-raising sessions, for example, we have in many ways gone beyond white women's revelations because we are dealing with the implications of race and class as well as sex. Even our black women's style of talking/testifying in black language about what we have experienced has a resonance that is both cultural and political. We have spent a great deal of energy delving into the cultural and experiential nature of our oppression out of necessity because none of these matters have ever been looked at before. No one before has ever examined the multilayered texture of black women's lives.

As we have already stated, we reject the stance of lesbian separatism because it is not a viable political analysis of strategy for us. It leaves out far too much and far too many people, particularly black men, women, and children. We have a great deal of criticism and loathing for what men have been socialized to be in this society: what they support, how they act, and how they oppress. But we do not have the misguided notion that it is their maleness, per se—i.e., their biological maleness—that makes them what they are. As black women we find any type of biological determinism a particularly dangerous and reactionary basis upon which to build a politic. We must also question whether lesbian separatism is an adequate and progressive political analysis and strategy, even for those who practice it, since it so completely denies any but the sexual sources of women's oppression, negating the facts of class and race. . . .

Black Feminist Issues and Practice

During our time together we have identified and worked on many issues of particular relevance to black women. The inclusiveness of our politics makes us concerned with any situation that impinges upon the lives of women, Third World, and working people. We are of course particularly committed to working on those struggles in which race, sex, and class are simultaneous factors in oppression. We might, for example, become involved in workplace organizing at a factory that employs Third World women, or picket a hospital that is cutting back on already inadequate health care to a Third World community, or set up a rape crisis center in a black neighborhood. Organizing around welfare or day-care concerns might also be a focus. The work to be done and the countless issues that this work represents merely reflect the pervasiveness of our oppression.

Issues and projects that collective members have actually worked on are sterilization abuse, abortion rights, battered women, rape, and health care. We have also done many workshops and educationals on black feminism on college campuses, at women's conferences, and most recently for high school women.

One issue that is of major concern to us and that we have begun to publicly address is racism in the white women's movement. As black feminists, we are made constantly and painfully aware of how little effort white women have made to understand and combat their racism, which requires among other things that they have a more than superficial comprehension of race, color, and black history and culture. Eliminating racism in the white women's movement is by definition work for white women to do, but we will continue to speak to and demand accountability on this issue.

In the practice of our politics we do not believe that the end always justifies the means. Many reactionary and destructive acts have been done in the name of achieving "correct" political goals. As feminists we do not want to mess over people in the name of politics. We believe in collective process and a nonhierarchical distribution of power within our own group and in our vision of a revolutionary society. We are committed to a continual examination of our politics as they develop through criticism and self-criticism as an essential aspect of our practice. As black feminists and lesbians, we know that we have a very definite revolutionary task to perform, and we are ready for the lifetime of work and struggle before us.

28. HARVEY MILK

The Hope Speech
(1978)

HARVEY MILK (1930–1978), the first openly gay elected politician in American history, has become the iconic martyr of the modern LGBT liberation movement. Born in Woodmere, New York, Milk's early life was shaped by middle-class convention. Increasingly, he was swept up in the hippie counterculture, sexual awakening, and radical ferment of the 1960s and 1970s. In 1972, he joined the large migration of gays and lesbians to San Francisco, where he managed a small camera store in the heart of the city's Castro District. In 1977, after three failed attempts, Milk made history when he was elected to the San Francisco Board of Supervisors. A master of both grassroots politics and media spectacle, Milk garnered support from unlikely constituencies— especially organized labor—who helped propel him to victory in his fourth and final campaign. Though his popularity grew over time—he was widely known as the "Mayor of Castro Street"—Milk was nonetheless a controversial figure, due to his outspoken opposition to Anita Bryant's 1977 "Save Our Children" campaign in Miami, Florida, and to subsequent efforts by California state senator John Briggs to pass a proposition barring gays and lesbians from teaching in public schools (the measure was ultimately defeated). Over time, Milk developed something of an obsession with his own mortality, even going so far as to record the following in an audiotaped will: "If a bullet should enter my brain, let that bullet destroy every closet door." Tragically, the first part of this prophecy would come to pass on November 27, 1978, when Milk and San Francisco Mayor George Moscone were gunned down by former fellow supervisor Dan White, an anti-gay conservative who resented Milk and Moscone's support of him. (White was given a shockingly light sentence—for manslaughter, he was acquitted of the murders—after which he committed suicide.) Milk's assassination cut short the promising career of a truly gifted gay rights advocate, but his example of hope—so evident in this political stump speech which he delivered on numerous occasions—continues to inspire LGBT activists and allies working to achieve a more free, equal, and just world.

SOURCE: Randy Shilts, *The Mayor of Castro Street: The Life and Times of Harvey Milk*. New York: St. Martin's Press, 1982.

SELECTED READINGS/FILMS: Randy Shilts, *The Mayor of Castro Street: The Life and Times of Harvey Milk* (1982); Adam Nagourney and Dudley Clendinen, *Out for Good: The Struggle to Build a Gay Rights Movement in America* (1999); Eric Marcus, *Making Gay History* (2002); *The Times of Harvey Milk* (dir. Rob Epstein, 1984); *Milk* (dir. Gus Van Sant, 2008).

My name is Harvey Milk and I'm here to recruit you.

I've been saving this one for years. It's a political joke. I can't help it—I've got to tell it. I've never been able to talk to this many political people before, so if I tell you nothing else you may be able to go home laughing a bit.

This ocean liner was going across the ocean and it sank. And there was one little piece of wood floating and three people swam to it and they realized only one person could hold on to it. So they had a little debate about which was the person. It so happened the three people were the Pope, the President, and Mayor Daley. The Pope said he was titular head of one of the great religions of the world and he was spiritual adviser to many, many millions and he went on and pontificated and they thought it was a good argument. Then the President said he was leader of the largest and most powerful nation of the world. What takes place in this country affects the whole world and they thought that was a good argument. And Mayor Daley said he was mayor of the backbone of the United States and what took place in Chicago affected the world and what took place in the archdiocese of Chicago affected Catholicism. And they thought that was a good argument. So they did it the democratic way and voted. And Daley won, seven to two.

About six months ago, Anita Bryant in her speaking to God said that the drought in California was because of the gay people. On November 9, the day after I got elected, it started to rain. On the day I got sworn in, we walked to City Hall and it was kinda nice, and as soon as I said the words "I do," it started to rain again. It's been raining since then and the people of San Francisco figure the only way to stop it is to do a recall petition. That's a local joke.

So much for that. Why are we here? Why are gay people here? And what's happening? What's happening to me is the antithesis of what you read about in the papers and what you hear about on the radio. You hear about and read about this movement to the right. That we must band together and fight back this movement to the right. And I'm here to go ahead and say that what you hear and read is what they want you to think because it's not happening. The major media in this country has talked about the movement to the right so much that they've got even us thinking that way. Because they want the legislators to think that there is indeed a movement to the right and that the Congress and the legislators and the city councils will start to move to the right the way the major media want them. So they keep on talking about this move to the right.

So let's look at 1977 and see if there was indeed a move to the right. In 1977, gay people had their rights taken away from them in Miami. But you must remember that in the week before Miami and the week after that, the word homosexual or gay appeared in every single newspaper in this nation in articles both pro and con. In every radio station, in every TV station and every household. For the first time in the history of the world, everybody was talking about it, good or bad. Unless you have dialogue, unless you open the walls of dialogue, you can never reach to change people's opinion. In those two weeks, more good and bad, but *more* about the words homosexual and gay was written than probably in the history of mankind. Once you have dialogue starting, you know you can break down the prejudice. In 1977, we saw a dialogue start. In 1977, we saw a gay person elected in San Francisco. In 1977, we saw the state of Mississippi decriminalize marijuana. In 1977, we saw the convention of conventions in Houston. And I want to know where the movement to the right is happening.

What that is is a record of what happened last year. What we must do is make sure that 1978 continues the movement that is really happening that the media don't want you to know about, that is the movement to the left. It's up to CDC to put the pressures on Sacramento—not to just bring flowers to Sacramento—but to break down the walls and the barriers so the movement to the left continues and progress continues in the nation. We have before us coming up several issues we must speak out on. Probably the most important issue outside the Briggs—which we will come to—but we do know what will take place this June. We know there's an issue on the ballot called Jarvis-Gann. We hear the taxpayers talk about it on both sides. But what you don't hear is that it's probably the most racist issue on the ballot in a long time. In the city and county of San Francisco, if it passes, and we indeed have to lay off people, who will they be? The last in, not the first in, and who are the last in but the minorities? Jarvis-Gann is a racist issue. We must address that issue. We must not talk away from it. We must not allow them to talk about the money it's going to save, because look at who's going to save the money and who's going to get hurt.

We also have another issue that we've started in some of the north counties, and I hope in some of the south counties it continues. In San Francisco elections we're asking—at least we hope to ask—that the U.S. government put pressure on the closing of the South African consulate. That must happen. There is a major difference between an embassy in Washington, which is a diplomatic bureau, and a consulate in major cities. A consulate is there for one reason only—to promote business, economic gains, tourism, investment. And every time you have business going to South Africa, you're promoting a regime that's offensive.

In the city of San Francisco, if every one of 51 percent of that city were to go to South Africa, they would be treated as second-class citizens. That is an offense to the people of San Francisco and I hope all my colleagues up there will take every step we can to close down that consulate, and [I] hope that people in other parts of the state follow us in that lead. The battles must be started some place, and CDC is the greatest place to start the battles.

I know we are pressed for time so I'm going to cover just one more little point. That is to understand why it is important that gay people run for office and that gay people get elected. I know there are many people in this room who are running for central committee who are gay. I encourage you. There's a major reason why. If my non-gay friends and supporters in this room understand it, they'll probably understand why I've run so often before I finally made it. Y'see right now, there's a controversy going on in this convention about the governor. Is he speaking out enough? Is he strong enough for gay rights? And there is a controversy, and for us to say it is not would be foolish. Some people are satisfied and some people are not.

You see there is a major difference—and it remains a vital difference—between a friend and a gay person, a friend in office and a gay person in office. Gay people have been slandered nationwide. We've been tarred and we've been brushed with the picture of pornography. In Dade County, we were accused of child molestation. It's not enough anymore just to have friends represent us. No matter how good that friend may be.

The black community made up its mind to that a long time ago. That the myths against blacks can only be dispelled by electing black leaders, so the black community could be judged by the leaders and not by the myths or black criminals. The Spanish community must not be judged by Latin criminals or myths. The Asian community must not be judged by Asian criminals or myths. The Italian community should not be judged by the mafia, myths. And the time has come when the gay community must not be judged by our criminals and myths.

Like every other group, we must be judged by our leaders and by those who are themselves gay, those who are visible. For invisible, we remain in limbo—a myth, a person with no parents, no brothers, no sisters, no friends who are straight, no important positions in employment. A tenth of a nation supposedly composed of stereotypes and would-be seducers of children—and no offense meant to the stereotypes. But today, the black community is not judged by its friends, but by its black legislators and leaders. And we must give people the chance to judge us by our leaders and legislators. A gay person in office can set a tone, can command respect not only from the larger community, but from the young people in our own community who need both examples and hope.

The first gay people we elect must be strong. They must not be content to sit in the back of the bus. They must not be content to accept pablum. They must be above wheeling and dealing. They must be—for the good of all of us—independent, unbought. The anger and the frustrations that some of us feel is because we are misunderstood, and friends can't feel that anger and frustration. They can sense it in us, but they can't feel it. Because a friend has never gone through what is known as coming out. I will never forget what it was like coming out and having nobody to look up toward. I remember the lack of hope—and our friends can't fulfill that.

I can't forget the looks on faces of people who've lost hope. Be they gay, be they seniors, be they blacks looking for an almost-impossible job, be they Latinos trying to explain their problems and aspirations in a tongue that's foreign to them. I personally will never forget that people are more important than buildings. I use the word "I" because I'm proud. I stand here tonight in front of my gay sisters, brothers, and friends because I'm proud of you. I think it's time that we have many legislators who are gay and proud of that fact and do not have to remain in the closet. I think that a gay person, up-front, will not walk away from a responsibility and be afraid of being tossed out of office. After Dade County, I walked among the angry and the frustrated night after night and I looked at their faces. And in San Francisco, three days before Gay Pride Day, a person was killed just because he was gay. And that night, I walked among the sad and the frustrated at City Hall in San Francisco and later that night as they lit candles on Castro Street and stood in silence, reaching out for some symbolic thing that would give them hope. These were strong people, people whose faces I knew from the shop, the streets, meetings, and people whom I never saw before but I knew. They were strong, but even they needed hope.

And the young gay people in the Altoona, Pennsylvanias, and the Richmond, Minnesotas, who are coming out and hear Anita Bryant on television and her story. The only thing they have to look forward to is hope. And you have to give them hope. Hope for a better world, hope for a better tomorrow, hope for a better place to come to if the pressures at home are too great. Hope that all will be alright. Without hope, not only gays, but the blacks, the seniors, the handicapped, the us'es, the us'es will give up. And if you help elect to the central committee and other offices more gay people, that gives a green light to all who feel disenfranchised, a green light to move forward. It means hope to a nation that has given up, because if a gay person makes it, the doors are open to everyone.

So if there is a message I have to give, it is that if I've found one overriding thing about my personal election, it's the fact that if a gay person can be elected, it's a green light. And you and you and you, you have to give people hope. Thank you very much.

29. AUDRE LORDE

The Master's Tools Will Never Dismantle
the Master's House
(1979)

AUDRE LORDE (1934–1992) was a writer, educator, and activist who described herself as a "black, lesbian, mother, warrior, poet." Born in New York City to West Indian immigrant parents, Lorde studied at Hunter College and Columbia University before settling in the vibrant bohemian community of Greenwich Village in the 1950s and 1960s, where she first began to explore her lesbian sexuality. During her early career, she held a series of working-class jobs, then served as a librarian, and finally secured several prominent academic posts, first as a writer-in-residence at Tougaloo College in Mississippi (where she met her longterm lover Frances Clayton), then as a professor at Hunter College and the John Jay College of Criminal Justice. She was the poet laureate of New York in 1991–92. As a poet, essayist, and novelist, Lorde used her writing to explore themes of "intersectionality"—the reality that we all are shaped by multiple identities of race, class, gender, sexuality, and nationality. She began her career as a poet, and her third book of poems, *From a Land Where Other People Live* (1973), was nominated for a National Book Award. Throughout the 1970s and 1980s, Lorde established herself as a gifted and prolific writer. She is perhaps best known for her "biomythography" *Zami: A New Spelling of My Name* (1982); a collection of speeches and essays, *Sister Outsider* (1984); and *A Burst of Light* (1988), which won the National Book Award. Today, her writings are often included in college courses in African-American, Women's, and

Queer Studies. Lorde wrote passionately about her struggle with breast cancer in *The Cancer Journals* (1980), her first prose collection. In 1992, at the age of just 58, she succumbed to the disease. The following essay, from *Sister Outsider*, powerfully articulates Lorde's approach to intersectionality, challenging white feminists, especially, to confront and uproot the various prejudices they have inherited—the "master's tools"—that prevent all women from joining in common cause across lines of difference to combat the multiple oppressions of racism, classism, sexism, and homophobia.

SOURCE: Audre Lorde, *Sister Outsider: Essays and Speeches by Audre Lorde.* Freedom, CA: The Crossing Press, 1984

SELECTED READINGS: Audre Lorde, *Sister Outsider: Essays and Speeches by Audre Lorde* (1984); Alexis De Veaux, *Warrior Poet: A Biography of Audre Lorde* (1996); Joan Wylie Hall, *Conversations with Audre Lorde* (2004); AnaLouise Keating, *Women Reading, Women Writing: Self-Invention in Paula Gunn Allen, Gloria Anzaldua, and Audre Lorde* (1996).

I agreed to take part in a New York University Institute for the Humanities conference a year ago, with the understanding that I would be commenting upon papers dealing with the role of difference within the lives of American women: difference of race, sexuality, class, and age. The absence of these considerations weakens any feminist discussion of the personal and the political.

It is a particular academic arrogance to assume any discussion of feminist theory without examining our many differences, and without a significant input from poor women, Black and Third World women, and lesbians. And yet, I stand here as a Black lesbian feminist, having been invited to comment within the only panel at this conference where the input of Black feminists and lesbians is represented. What this says about the vision of this conference is sad, in a country where racism, sexism, and homophobia are inseparable. To read this program is to assume that lesbian and Black women have nothing to say about existentialism, the erotic, women's culture and silence, developing feminist theory, or heterosexuality and power.

And what does it mean in personal and political terms when even the two Black women who did present here were literally found at the last hour? What does it mean when the tools of a racist patriarchy are used to examine the fruits of that same patriarchy? It means that only the most narrow parameters of change are possible and allowable.

The absence of any consideration of lesbian consciousness or the consciousness of Third World women leaves a serious gap within this conference and within the papers presented here. For example, in a paper on material relationships between women, I was conscious of an either-or model of nurturing which totally dismissed my knowledge as a Black lesbian. In this paper there was no examination of mutuality between women, no systems of shared support, no interdependence as exists between lesbians and women-identified women. Yet it is only in the patriarchal model of nurturance that women "who attempt to emancipate themselves pay perhaps too high a price for the results," as this paper states.

For women, the need and desire to nurture each other is not pathological but redemptive, and it is within that knowledge that our real power is rediscovered. It is this real connection which is so feared by a patriarchal world. Only within a patriarchal structure is maternity the only social power open to women.

Interdependency between women is the way to a freedom which allows the I to be, not in order to be used, but in order to be creative. This is a difference between the passive be and the active being.

Advocating the mere tolerance of difference between women is the grossest reformism. It is a total denial of the creative function of difference in our lives. Difference must be not merely tolerated, but seen as a fund of necessary polarities between which our creativity can spark like a dialectic. Only then does the necessity for interdependency become unthreatening. Only within that interdependency of different strengths, acknowledged and equal, can the power to seek new ways of being in the world generate, as well as the courage and sustenance to act where there are no charters.

Within the interdependence of mutual (nondominant) differences lies that security which enables us to descend into the chaos of knowledge and return with true visions of our future, along with the concomitant power to effect those changes which can bring that future into being. Difference is that raw and powerful connection from which our personal power is forged.

As women, we have been taught either to ignore our differences or to view them as causes for separation and suspicion rather than as forces for change. Without community there is no liberation, only the most vulnerable and temporary armistice between an individual and her oppression. But community must not mean a shedding of our differences, nor the pathetic pretense that these differences do not exist.

Those of us who stand outside the circle of this society's definition of acceptable women; those of us who have been forged in the crucibles of difference—those of us who are poor, who are lesbians, who are Black, who are older—know that *survival is not an academic skill.* It is learning how to stand alone, unpopular and sometimes reviled, and how to make common cause with those others identified as outside the structures in order to define and seek a world in which we can all flourish. It is learning how to take our differences and make them strengths. *For the master's tools will never dismantle the master's house.* They may allow us temporarily to beat him at his own game, but they will never enable us to bring about genuine change. And this fact is only threatening to those women who still define the master's house as their only source of support.

Poor women and women of Color know there is a difference between the daily manifestations of marital slavery and prostitution because it is our daughters who line 42nd Street. If white American feminist theory need not deal with the differences between us, and the resulting difference in our oppressions, then how do you deal with the fact that the women who clean your houses and tend your children while you attend conferences on feminist theory are, for the most part, poor women and women of Color? What is the theory behind racist feminism?

In a world of possibility for us all, our personal visions help lay the groundwork for political action. The failure of academic feminists to recognize difference as a crucial strength is a failure to reach beyond the first patriarchal lesson. In our world, divide and conquer must become define and empower.

Why weren't other women of Color found to participate in this conference? Why were two phone calls to me considered a consultation? Am I the only possible source of names of Black feminists? And although the Black panelist's paper ends on an important and powerful connection of love between women, what about interracial cooperation between feminists who don't love each other?

In academic feminist circles, the answer to these questions is often, "We did not know who to ask." But that is the same evasion of responsibility, the same cop-out, that keeps Black women's art out of women's exhibitions, Black women's work out of most feminist publications except for the occasional "Special Third World Women's Issue," and Black women's texts off your reading lists. But, as Adrienne Rich pointed out in a recent talk, white feminists have educated themselves about such an enormous amount over the past ten years, how come you haven't also educated yourselves about Black women and the differences between us—white and Black—when it is key to our survival as a movement?

Women of today are still being called upon to stretch across the gap of male ignorance and to educate men as to our existence and our needs. This is an old and primary tool of all oppressors to keep the oppressed occupied with the master's concerns. Now we hear that it is the task of women of Color to educate white women—in the face of tremendous resistance—as to our existence, our differences, our relative roles in our joint survival. This is a diversion of energies and a tragic repetition of racist patriarchal thought.

Simone de Beauvoir once said: "It is in the knowledge of the genuine conditions of our lives that we must draw our strength to live and our reasons for acting."

Racism and homophobia are real conditions of all our lives in this place and time. *I urge each one of us here to reach down into that deep place of knowledge inside herself and touch that terror and loathing of any difference that lives there. See whose face it wears.* Then the personal as the political can begin to illuminate all our choices.

Permissions

We are grateful for permission to reproduce the following copyrighted material (in cases where copyright information is omitted for works not in the public domain, every effort has been made to contact the copyright holders; any omissions will be corrected in subsequent reprintings):

Excerpt from "An Obligation to Endure" from *Silent Spring* by Rachel Carson. Copyright © 1962 by Rachel L. Carson, renewed 1990 by Roger Christie. Reprinted by permission of Houghton Mifflin Company. All rights reserved.

"Letter from Delano" by César Chávez, from the April 23, 1969 issue of *The Christian Century*. Reprinted by permission of The César Chávez Foundation.

Excerpt from "Political Prisoners, Prisons, and Black Liberation" by Angela Y. Davis from Angela Y. Davis, ed., *If They Come in the Morning: Voices of Resistance* (New York: Third Press, 1971). Copyright © 1971 by Angela Y. Davis. Reprinted by permission of the author.

Excerpt from *The Feminine Mystique* by Betty Friedan. Copyright © 1983, 1974, 1973, 1963, by Betty Friedan. Used by permission of W.W. Norton & Company, Inc.

"Letter from Birminghan Jail" reprinted by arrangement with the Estate of Martin Luther King, Jr, c/o Writers House as agent for the